A Town Called Festive

"Hope, second chances and forgiveness"

Sandra Macauley

D0862086

Brighton Publishing LLC
435 N. Harris Drive
Mesa, AZ 85203

A TOWN CALLED FESTIVE
"HOPE, SECOND CHANCES AND FORGIVENESS"

SANDRA MACAULEY

BRIGHTON PUBLISHING LLC

435 N. HARRIS DRIVE

MESA, AZ 85203

WWW.BRIGHTONPUBLISHING.COM

ISBN: 978-1-62183-558-5

First Edition

COVER DESIGN BY TOM RODRIGUEZ

Acknowledgments

First and foremost, I would like to thank the Creator for answering my prayers.

To my family–I owe you so much for all the emotional support, prayers and encouragement that you all have given me through the years. I could not have done this without you. I hope you all know that I appreciate and love very much.

My friends Myra Nelson, Stacie Caviness, Vonda Brown, Tia, Mary Patterson, Tonya West. Thank you all for keeping things real and encouraging me to reach for the stars. I know you have prayed for me many times over the years. I appreciate your kindness and support.

Kent Jones–From Kent Jones photography Thank you for the pictures and making me look good. You are the best.

Jeanie Horn–Thank you for all you did to help me reach my dreams

The staff at Brighton publishing–Thank you for all for your hard work and making my dream a reality.

Dedication

I would like to dedicate this book to my Parents and my Grandparents. I love you all so very much. I miss you every day, and I hope you are looking down from heaven and smiling

"It was always said of him, that he knew how to keep Christmas well, if any man alive possessed the knowledge. May that be truly said of us, and all of us."

~Charles Dickens "A Christmas Carol"

Chapter One

The snow had accumulated about three inches deep outside the Memories Diner. Val admired the landscape while she adjusted the green holly garland that hung around the picture window. Then she turned to look around the diner, taking mental notes of what still had to be done before the Lights on Festival crowd this coming Saturday. The 1950's diner was red brick and mortar outside with a silver and red counter area, and black and white checked floors inside. Red leather covered chairs and silver and white tables gave a cheery Christmas look to the seating arrangement. Val grabbed her apron off the back of one of the chairs and tightened it around her waist. Blue jeans, blue flannel shirt and sneakers were a far cry from the all-white uniform she used to wear. She looked at the red and white clock above the jukebox and noticed it was almost 6:00 a.m. Just then the bell above the door jingled and startled her.

"Hey, I know I am running late," Amy said as she rushed in the door and started peeling off her green knit scarf. Amy's five foot three and chubby physic was covered by a brown wool coat. Her red hair peeked from the edges of her green hat.

"I expect we will have our usual customers today, and the crowds will start coming into town tomorrow for the first festival. I already got the coffee going and the breakfast casserole special pulled out of the fridge. I already peeled the potatoes for the hash browns," Val said.

"So, did you come into work at 2:00 a.m.?"

"No, I did some of the prep work yesterday after the Thanksgiving dinner at the church. Then Maggie and I watched a couple of Christmas movies."

"Where is Maggie today?"

"In my office sleeping on the couch. She is going to spend the day with her best friend."

"I still wish you two would have come to dinner with me and Ben. Even though his mother is the worst cook in all the United-States. I mean who puts broccoli in their stuffing." Amy hung her coat up on the coat stand by the front door. "She kept complaining about how her back hurt and how no one ever helps her with anything."

Amy walked toward the counter area. "I swear my eyes rolled so many times, I must have looked like a slot machine." Amy reached under the counter and pulled out a tray filled with salt and pepper shakers.

"Well, you could have been at the church with me and having to listen to Mr. Jeffers complain about everything from the church hall being too cold to the outfit Mrs. Grey wore." Val smiled.

"Okay, you win the dealing with cranky people contest."

"So, after you put out the salt and pepper shakers, please write out the specials on the chalkboard. I am going to get ready for the day. Don't forget to put on the sign that we are closing tomorrow at 5:00 p.m. Maybe Ben's Mom is so dramatic because she is lonely."

"Are you suggesting I get her a dog or a cat?"

"That is a thought."

Val grabbed her purse from under the counter and walked into the lady's room. Checking her make up in the mirror. *Not bad for all the road mileage.* She pulled bobby pins out of her purse, smoothed her long brown ponytail up into a bun and pinned it in place. She washed her hands, and then steadied herself against the vanity. She looked down into the sink, then back at the mirror, and took a deep breath.

"Okay, let's go."

James Hawk walked into the newspaper's office promptly at 8:00 a.m. The office was already filled with other reporters and their chatter grew silent as James made his way to his desk and sat down. James glanced around the room and saw everyone starring at him. He picked up the copy of yesterday's paper that someone put on his desk and saw that someone had circled the retraction in red that they were forced to print.

"It is not the end of the world you know." He said to the crowd.

His editor and chief Bryon Walker blasted open his office door. His short and round frame was stiff with anger. He wore a white shirt and blue pants. The color of his face matched his bright red Christmas tie.

"James, my office, now." Everyone else turned and watched James get up and walk towards his supervisor. "The rest of you get back to work."

"Maybe it is the end of the world," James whispered.

Bryon slammed the door after James entered the room. James stood in front of his boss's brown desk.

"Sit down, James," he ordered, and James slowly complied.

"All I wanted to do yesterday was spend a quiet Thanksgiving with my family and my baby granddaughter. But no and you know why."

"I have a feeling I do."

"I had to spend a great portion of time on the phone defending you to my boss and basically, trying to keep your job."

"My source," James started to defend himself but was cut off by his boss.

"Your source at the City Councils office turned out to be the one embezzling the money. Now the Chairman of the City Council wants your head."

"I admit, I got this one wrong, I can write up a story about how the source tried to cover their tracks by lying today."

"That has been done already. I don't think you realize how serious this is. The Mayor who is the brother of the Chairman is the one who called my boss."

"Am I fired?"

"No, but I am benching you until this thing blows over."

"Benching me? Bryon, you know why I need this job."

"Be grateful I am not firing you. I am sending you to a town called Festive. It is north of Frederick, Maryland. Apparently, they go crazy this time of year with Christmas festivals and spreading goodwill things."

"You're putting me on the style page?"

"Yeah, until you get your groove back, and be grateful you have a job. You need to leave today. The first festival is tomorrow. Take your camera because you're going to have to do own photography. You are booked on the four o'clock flight to Baltimore. See Jo Anne for the rest of your accommodations information."

James got up and headed for the door.

"James, do not mess this up, I won't be able to save your job again."

Forty-five minutes later James opened the front door to his mother's Chicago row house. He hung his coat up in the coat closet and headed into the living room, immediately noticing the many Christmas decoration filled boxes lining the couch.

"I told her I would get those boxes out of the attic," he whispered. He then turned to see his Mom walking down the stairs. She was wearing a red sweater with a light-up Christmas tree on it, black pants and white tennis shoes. Her graying hair was combed into a semi-Marilyn Monroe style.

"James, what are you doing home so early?"

"I have to pack for an assignment out of town."

"Where are you going?"

"Festive, Maryland."

"Is that the name of an actual town?"

"Yeah,"

"Who names a town Festive? That is just plain weird if you ask me."

James walked toward the kitchen and his mother followed. He got a mug out of the cabinet. "Do you want some coffee?"

5

"Nah, how long will you be gone?"

James grabbed the coffee pot from the coffee maker and filled his mug. "I did some research before I left work; it seems that they have several festivals this time of year. Right up till Christmas Eve."

"Christmas Eve."

"Don't worry, I should be home by then."

"That place sounds like some crazy tourists' spot to me."

"Well, maybe. Now tell me who got the Christmas decorations down from the attic."

"Harvey's nephew. He is visiting for the holidays. I casually mentioned to Harvey when he called this morning that you were working, so he sent his nephew over."

"You casually mentioned." James gave her the one eyebrow lifted look.

"I swear." She put her hand on her chest and raised her right hand.

"I am worried about leaving you here alone for so long."

"I got the canasta card group every Tuesday, Mrs. Shaffer comes over and complains about her kids. Harvey is over here all the time since his wife died. I am lucky to get a moment and take a breath."

"Okay, Mom. I better get packed."

"Don't forget to pack an extra set of gloves, you always lose your gloves."

Val had just finished putting the porcelain dolls in the diner storefront window when she spotted Mr. Jeffers walking toward the diner. He was about eighty-five years old and he wore a dark old brown wool coat, with a just as old brown hat and scarf. Val walked toward the front door and opened it for him.

"I can get the door myself," he said as he walked in.

"I know that." Val reached for his coat.

"Eh," he moaned. "I can hang up my own coat too." He hung his outer belongings up on the coat rack.

"All right then, I was beginning to wonder if you were coming in today. You are a little late."

"Darn tourists' traffic." He headed toward the counter.

Val smiled knowing he lived just across the street. She noticed that Mr. Jeffers' sweater and slacks were just a tad too big for his skinny frame.

"Amy," he yelled as he sat down.

"I'm coming," she said as she opened the swinging door carrying a brown tray filled with clean white coffee mugs. She put the tray on the counter. Then grabbed the coffee pot and filled one cup for Mr. Jeffers. "Here you go, Mr. Jeffers."

"Where is my cream and sugar?" he bellowed.

Amy pushed the cream and sugar container from the space next to Mr. Jeffers in his direction.

"Hard to get good help these days," he mumbled.

"Would you like your usual order of oatmeal, fresh fruit and toast or would you like to try something else today?"

"Amy, I have been getting the same breakfast every morning since she opened the place. So, stop asking me what I want and get on with it."

"Mr. Jeffers, you really need to be nice," Val interjected.

"Why? I am an old man and I have earned my right to be grumpy all the time."

"Mama, where are my tennis shoes?" Maggie yelled from the back office.

"Duty calls." Val walked toward the back room.

"Why is Maggie here?"

"Kids have today off from school," Amy answered.

"If that one had a husband she wouldn't have to worry about such things, she could be at home with her kids."

"Barefoot and pregnant?"

"Now you put words in my mouth."

"No, I have known you all of my life and your views on such topics are well documented."

"Bah, So I am old fashioned. Is that a crime now?"

Val opened the door to her office and found Maggie kneeling on the floor looking under the couch.

"Good morning pumpkin. Your shoes are next to your backpack."

"Oh, hi Mom," she said as she scrambled up off the floor.

Five-year-old Maggie had her favorite blue sweater and blue jeans on. Her light brown hair hung loosely around her face. She sat back down on the couch and put her shoes on.

"Angie's Mom is going to take you to the movies today. Your boots are next to your coat."

8

"Do I have to wear my boots? They are ugly."

"Yes, you must wear your boots, they keep your feet dry, so you won't get cold and sick. Now hand me your brush so I can pull your hair back."

"Is cranky Mr. Jeffers here?"

"Excuse me," Val spoke as she brushed her daughter's hair. "That is Mr. Jeffers to you, young lady, and yes he is here."

"Everyone calls him that."

"Yeah, but that is still impolite. So, don't do it."

"Yes, ma'am."

Val pulled her daughter's hair into a ponytail. "Okay, go wash your face and hands and I will make some French toast for your breakfast."

"Yes, ma'am."

"Maggie, I want you to sit next to Mr. Jeffers this morning and say hello and try to talk to him."

"About what?"

"What your plans are for today or what you have learned in school."

"Yes, ma'am." She looked down at the floor.

"A little kindness goes a long way, remember that."

"Yes, ma'am."

"Okay now go wash up."

Val walked over to the refrigerator and pulled out the eggs, strawberries, milk and bread for the French toast. She put the ingredients on the counter and then reached above the stove and pulled down the almond extract and powdered sugar. She dredged the bread in the egg, milk, and extract mix. While the bread was cooking, she pulled a large pot of turkey stock out of the refrigerator and put it on the stove. A few moments later she walked toward the door carrying her daughter's breakfast. Amy was clearing the dishes from some of the booth tables.

"Here you go pumpkin. Do you want orange juice or apple juice?"

"Can I have a soda instead?"

"No," Val laughed.

"Apple juice please."

Val reached under the counter and grabbed a glass.

"Do you like cranberries Mr. Jeffers?"

"I'm sorry what did you ask?"

"Do you like cranberries?"

"Well, yes I do." He acted a little taken aback by a five-year-old asking him a question.

Val put the glass of apple juice down next to her daughter's plate.

"My Mom is going to teach me how to make a Nantucket pie."

"Does it have cranberries in it?" he asked.

"Yes, sir and pecans. My Mom makes it every Christmas, but this year I get to help."

"That sounds good."

"Is Thomas coming in today?" Amy as she walked toward the counter.

"Who is Thomas?" Mr. Jeffers asked

"Val hired him to wash dishes and clean up."

"He should be here in about five minutes and you Miss have about ten minutes before Angie's Mom gets here. So, finish your breakfast, please."

"Yes, ma'am."

James arrived at the Holly Inn just before 8:00 p.m. He pulled into the parking lot and could not help but be struck by the beauty of the Inn.

"Currier and Ives has nothing on this place," he spoke out loud to himself.

According to the information James found on-line the white three-story mansion was converted to an Inn in the 1940s. The original place was first built during 1901. Each window had a wreath and red velvet bow hanging in front of it. The porch railing was lined with green garland and two big wreaths hung on the double front door. He got the luggage out of his rental car and started toward the front entrance.

He opened the front door and headed into the lobby area. He immediately noticed all the dark cherry colored wood along the floor and the massive stairway in front of him. To the right was the lobby desk. He walked over and saw the silver bell at the counter then reached out and tapped it.

"I will be right there." A female voice called out.

James surveyed the surroundings a little more while he waited. He noticed just beyond the lobby was an oval dining room, and in what must have been the formal room living there was a large fireplace. He walked to the other side of the hallway and he noticed a large room that had another sitting area at one end and a den area at the other.

"That used to be the ballroom." James swiveled around as he heard someone come up behind him.

"You must be James Hawk; my name is Rose McDonald. Welcome to the Holly Inn." Rose looked to him to be somewhere in her seventies. She had white hair and stood about five feet tall. She wore a bright red sweater and black pants.

"Yes, ma'am. I believe my newspaper made a reservation in my name." He handed her the company credit card.

"You lucked out; we had a last-minute cancellation. All the hotels and Inns fill up this time of year because of the activities going on in town. The Johnson family had an emergency."

That statement seemed a little odd to James. "Do you have many regulars this time of year?"

Oh yes, most of our customers have been coming here for many years. It has become a tradition for them. Like a big extended reunion of family and friends every year."

"I noticed you have a library."

"We have quite a collection of old and new novels, you can check out any book you would like."

"Thank you."

"Now we start serving breakfast at 6:00 a.m. in the dining room. You are in suite six. At the top of the stairs, the fourth door on the left."

"Is there a restaurant nearby? I drove here straight from the airport."

"Well, the Memories Diner may still be open. You make a right out of our parking lot and go about a mile down the road. It is right next to the barbershop."

"Thank you."

James pulled his luggage up the stairs and opened the massive door to his room. There was a large brass bed and an antique dresser in the room. There was a white quilt with red poinsettias covered the bed. The rose and white wallpaper reminded him of his grandmother's former home. By the window, there was a small table and a red upholstered Queen Anne style chair. His mother had a blue one in her bedroom. He could tell that the lamps in the room were also antiques. He walked into the bathroom and saw a large white clawfoot tub. He leaned over the white sink and splashed water on his face.

Val was wiping down the booth tables when she glanced back at the counter and noticed that Maggie was trying very hard to stay awake.

Chris came out of the backroom. He had on a black Nirvana tee shirt and blue jeans. He had a tattoo of a rose on his left forearm and a tattoo of a cross on the other arm. His twenty-five-year-old frame suggested he once had a hard life and attitude.

"I didn't think that last couple would ever leave," he said.

"Young couples in love tend to stay out as close as they can to their parent's curfew rules."

"You think they are in love?"

"It is easy to recognize high-school puppy love when you have been in this business for a while. Are all of the dishes done?"

"Yes," Chris noticed a man walking by the front entrance.

"Oh no, a last-minute customer," he moaned.

"I got this; you go on home," Val said.

"Nah, I'll stay." When Val looked at him, he added, "There is safety in numbers."

"You are talking about Festive, Maryland, not New York."

"You're the one from New York" Chris reminded her.

Through a window James noticed the two of them inside the restaurant. "Memories Diner, great greasy food," he muttered as he opened the door.

"Are you still open?" he asked.

"Yes," Val answered She turned and immediately tall and handsome, James was. He wore a camel-colored coat and blue jeans; His long black hair was pulled back into a ponytail. *He has got to be Native American.*

"We were about to close," Chris muttered.

James stayed in his spot close to the door. "Oh, I just got here from Chicago and Rose at the Holly Inn recommended this place."

"Well, I guess we can't turn away a weary traveler." Val answered. "So why don't you have a seat at the counter and Chris will get you a menu. You can hang your coat on the rack if you would like."

When he took off his coat, Val noticed how nice he looked in his white button-down shirt. *Okay brain calm down.*

James sat down a few seats away from Maggie, asleep with her head on the counter. Chris handed him a menu.

Val walked over toward Maggie reached out and tapped her weary daughters' shoulder. "Come on sleepyhead. Let's go back to the office for a little bit."

"Is it time to go home yet?"

"Not just yet." Val carried her daughter towards the office.

James scanned the menu and was surprised to see turkey tortilla soup with chorizo on the menu.

"What would you like to drink?" Chris asked.

"I'll take an unsweet iced-tea, and I have the turkey-tortilla soup with chorizo and a side salad."

"What type of dressing do you want?"

"What do you have?"

"Ranch, Thousand Island, French, Catalina, and Italian."

"Catalina."

"Okay, I'll have it out for you in just a moment."

Chris walked toward the kitchen.

James looked around the diner and he noticed a red and white clock on one of the walls hanging above a vintage jukebox. On another wall above one of the booths, hung a picture frame and instead of holding a painting, behind the glass were various postcards from all over the world. From his vantage point, he recognized the pictures of London Bridge, Blarney Castle and the Eiffel Tower.

Val walked in carrying his iced tea, and immediately noticed him starring at the postcards "Some of those are mine and others are from customers. Would you like lemon with your tea?"

"No thank you. Does your jukebox work?"

"Of course, it does. I had it converted to use CDs"

"Which postcards are yours?"

"The one from Blarney Castle, Carmel California, Cuenca Spain, Dublin Ireland, and Disney World. Are you in town for the festivals?"

"Yes, I understand there are a lot of them between now and New Year's."

"Fourteen to be exact. Starting tomorrow night with the Lights on Festival"

"Lights on?"

"Everyone turns on their outside lights tomorrow night and there is a festival at the park. Various choral groups and vendors will be there to start off the holidays. There are huge light displays and of course food."

Chris walked out of the kitchen carrying the soup and salad and placed the items in front of James.

"It sorts of sounds like a tourist gimmick."

"That tells me for sure you have never been here before," Val answered.

"No, I haven't."

"Well then I guess you will have to see what this town is really about, sir."

"My name is James: James Hawk" He swallowed a spoonful of soup. "Wow, this is terrific. I can see why Rose recommended this place."

"Thank you, my name is Val, and this is Chris. Rose is one of my best customers. I am going to check on my daughter. Chris, why don't you get a bag of the Mexican wedding cookies for this gentleman, the treat is on the house."

"Thank you."

"You're welcome, sir."

"James"

"Okay, James."

James looked up at Chris who had his arms folded and was staring at him.

"Are you two married?' James asked.

"No, But I am very protective of my friends," Chris replied.

ᚑ Chapter Two ᚑ

V al stood outside of the diner the next morning watching Ben up on the ladder attaching white Christmas lights to the frame of the brick building.

"How does this look?" Ben asked.

"Fine, I am going to get the wreath and I will be right back." Val heard a car pull up and park behind her. She turned and noticed James getting out of a tan color sedan.

"Good morning," she said. "Are you lost? The festival doesn't start until tonight."

"I heard you have a great breakfast and since I overslept and missed the one at the inn this morning."

"Come on in and we will get you set up."

"Don't forget me, it is cold out here," Ben yelled.

"I will be right back"

James held the door open for Val and she walked in. She noticed her daughter sitting next to Mr. Jeffers who was almost finished eating his oatmeal breakfast.

"Why don't you hang your coat up and have a seat at the counter? Amy will take your order."

Val walked over to the counter area as Amy was ringing up a customer.

"Thanks for stopping by Mr. Jacobs, will we see you tonight at the festival?" Amy asked

"Of course, my grandkids arrived last night. I can't wait to take them." He answered.

"Amy," Val started. "This is Mr. Hawk. He is a first-time visitor to our town. I have to get the wreath for Ben."

James sat down in a seat next to Maggie.

"After Ben finishes here, he has to go to the hardware store and put their decorations up and then he has to go over to the park and finish putting up their display," Amy added.

"I better get moving then." Val went through the kitchen door, walked past the cooking area, and opened her office door. She opened the large box she had placed on the couch earlier that morning, pulled the wreath out and stared at it for a moment. She looked away, attempting to blink back a tear. *Don't let Maggie see you cry.* She opened the office door and headed out to the main area.

"Mr. Hawk, our specials include two eggs, corned beef hash which is made with real corned beef, not the canned stuff, and toast. We also have pumpkin pancakes or French toast stuffed with raspberries and white chocolate sauce."

Val headed past them as Amy was finishing up the specials list.

"I'll have the corned beef special with the eggs over easy and the wheatberry bread toast. Plus, a cup of coffee."

Val opened the door and handed Ben the wreath.

"See I didn't forget you. When you are done come inside and I'll fix breakfast for you. On the house."

"Thank you and where do you want the wreath?

"Center it above the window." Val headed inside.

Amy handed her James order as she walked toward the counter.

"You were right, he is cute," Amy whispered.

"You're taken remember,"

"I can still look."

"What will Ben want for breakfast?"

"The pumpkin pancakes with sausage."

"I got these orders, and can you get Maggie a hot chocolate please."

"Done."

Val headed toward the kitchen while Amy pulled a mug out from under the counter and she poured in the hot chocolate and topped it with real whipped cream, not the stuff from an air puffed can or a plastic tub.

"Mr. Jeffers, are you going to the festival tonight?" Maggie asked.

Mr. Jeffers cleared his throat. "No, I am too old for those things."

"My Mom is going to take me this year. Today I am going over to the library with my friend Beth, so we can make Christmas cards."

"That sounds like fun."

"Do you decorate your house?"

"I put a candle in my window and a wreath on my door." He huffed a little.

"That's nice. Mom already put the lights on our outside Christmas tree and around the roof. Then she put a candle in every window and the green stuff on our fence."

"The green stuff is called garland," Mr. Jeffers corrected her.

"Yes, sir. Do you put up and decorate a Christmas tree?"

"No. Your hot chocolate is getting cold."

Maggie took a sip of her drink. James smiled. "Inquisitive children," he whispered.

"Orders up," Val said as she put two plates on the back counter.

Amy turned around and got James' order. She turned again and placed it in front of him. "Is there anything else I can get you?"

"I was wondering, is there a schedule of the festivals printed anywhere."

"Yeah, there are a couple by the register. I'll get a copy for you in just a minute."

Amy started for the front door just as Ben walked in. She hugged his tall skinny frame and then grabbed his brown hat off his head and put it on the coat rack shelf.

"Hang your coat up, your breakfast is ready."

"I got the wreath up. I hope it is centered like Ms. Val wanted." Ben hung up his coat and headed toward the counter. He sat down next to James, who nodded a hello and Ben nodded back.

"I am sure it is fine." Amy grabbed a copy of the schedule and handed it to James.

"Are you in town for the light festival?" Ben asked James.

James was a little taken aback by Ben being friendly and starting a conversation.

"Yes, I am, in fact I may be here for all of them."

Val was cleaning off the grill preparing for the lunch menu when she heard the backdoor open. She looked up and saw Thomas walking in the door. She noticed that he was not wearing a hat and that his blue coat was threadbare and not suitable for the winter weather. His black curly hair had some snowflakes in it. Val had heard from Rose that Thomas's mother was working as a custodian at the school and that she was having a hard time keeping her five children clothed and fed since her husband left her.

"Good morning. Is it starting to snow again?"

"Yes, ma'am."

"Have you eaten your breakfast yet?"

Thomas looked at his feet and shrugged his shoulders.

"Go sit at the counter and I'll bring you some breakfast."

Thomas looked down at his feet again.

"Thomas, what is it?"

"I am not dressed up," he answered. "I just have a tee shirt and jeans on."

"Everyone is welcomed here. But if it will make you feel better, I will make you a breakfast sandwich and you can eat it in my office. Now in the meantime go hang your coat up and pick up the tubs of dirty dishes Amy has under the counter."

"Yes, Ma'am."

Thomas walked through the kitchen door and headed toward the coat rack. Mr. Jeffers noticed him as he walked by. He shook his head and watched Thomas make his way back toward the kitchen area.

"Who is that?" Mr. Jeffers asked. In his gruff filled voice

"That is Thomas, he is the extra dishwasher Val hired," Amy answered.

"He looks a little rough to me."

"Every teenager looks rough to you," Val said as she walked into the room. "However, this particular teenager is a straight-A student and is working here to help out his Mom. So be nice." Val turned her attention towards Maggie. "Baby girl, your ride will be here in a few minutes, so go get your backpack please."

Maggie slid off the stool. "Bye Mr. Jeffers."

"Goodbye, Maggie."

Mr. Jeffers put the cash for his meal on the counter and got up slowly. As he put his coat, hat and scarf on Val walked over to the door and held it open for him. "All of us have our struggles especially the young ones, who don't have the wisdom or experience that we old ones do." She tightened his scarf. "Be careful out there it started snowing again."

"You are only in your thirties, and who are you calling old." He grumbled his way out the door.

"Where is a good place to park for the festival tonight?" James asked Ben.

"You may want to park in the lot behind the gazebo." Ben answered

"There will be dozens of food vendors there, games, raffles, music, and after the mayor gives a speech, he officially turns on the lights," Amy added.

"Yeah, this year I put up the toy section," Ben added. "We have giant light displays in the shape of toys; there is a teddy bear that is so high we have to use a crane to put that up. Then there is the jack in the box display and the lighted bicycle. There are seven different theme areas this year."

"Yes." Val said. "Let's see if I remember them, the reindeer school, Frosty the snowman, the aforementioned toy section, the old English village, Santa's castle, the Christmas bakery, and I forgot the other one."

"The North Pole animal section." Ben added.

"This all starts at 7:00 p.m." James asked.

"Well sort of," Amy answered. All businesses and homeowners turn their lights on at 6:00 p.m."

"Still sounds like a tourist trap to me."

"Stick around and you may learn what our town is really about." Val started. "Amy, I forgot to add rockfish stuffed with crabmeat to the specials today, can you put that on the board for me? I have to go check on my daughter."

"What type of diner has stuffed rockfish on the menu?" James asked.

"You should be here on the days she cooks her famous crab dinner. She makes the best soup and crab cakes they are outstanding. The line of people waiting to get in here goes around the block."

"Interesting," James said.

"Ben, you need to get moving or you will be late."

"All right, I will call you later Amy," he turned to James and put out his hand.

"Nice meeting you."

James shook his hand. "Same here."

After finishing his breakfast and paying his bill, James decided to take a stroll along Main Street. At first glance, the downtown area didn't seem much different than other small towns. There was the bank, hardware store and various other shops. There was a movie theater and an old brick building with white pillars that housed the Chamber of Commerce. Various shapes of row homes filled the empty spaces. However, it was the action occurring on the streets that told the real story. Shop owners, businesspeople, and families were putting the final touches on their outdoor decorations. The candy store had red-and-white lights around the window and giant fake candy canes by the front door. A group of people where decorating the Christmas tree in front of the Chamber of Commerce building. He turned and noticed a man in a suit directing workers on how to hang the large wreath on the bank building.

"Hey James," James looked up and saw Ben on the roof of the hardware store. He was adjusting the lights next to the giant Santa sleigh. "What do you think?"

James smiled and gave him a thumbs' up.

Someone had placed large wreaths with red ribbons on each of the old-fashioned streetlights.

James turned and starting walking back toward his car. As he approached his car door, he looked across the street and saw Mr. Jeffers gently putting a well-worn silver wreath on his door. He noticed that Mr. Jeffers stared at it for a moment and then the older gentleman went inside his house.

"This has got to be all a gimmick," he whispered as he opened his car door and got inside.

James pulled into the parking lot of the Inn and noticed Rose and a gentleman wrapping Christmas lights around the white wooden poles on the front porch. He walked toward Rose.

"Good afternoon," he said.

"Good afternoon to you too, Mr. Hawk." She motioned towards her husband who was about to get up on the wooden ladder. "Hal, this is James Hawk. He is staying with us for a while. This is my husband, Hal." Hal appeared to be in his seventies also, he was thin, with silver hair just below the trim of his red and black checkered wool winter hat.

"Do you need help with that?" James asked.

"Well young man, if you could just attach the lights to the hook at the top of the pole, I can do the rest," Hal said.

James got up on the old ladder and immediately felt how unsteady it was. Hal handed him the lights and James saw a small silver hook on the back of the pole. After attaching the lights, he got off the ladder. "Are you putting lights on the other poles? James pointed to the ones on the porch.

"Yes," Hal answered.

"Well, how about I get those started for you, so you don't have to climb the ladder."

"Deal," Hal said.

"Well, I am going inside and make the mulled wine for later tonight," Rose said. "After you are done here, Mr. Hawk. Why don't you come inside? There is a pot of hot coffee in the lobby area and some sugar cookies and other snacks."

"Thank you."

26

Half an hour later both Hal and James walked into the lobby. There was a couple with two children sitting in the main living room. The boy appeared to James to be about five years old and the girl looked to be around three years old. Hal walked over to them and the couple stood up.

"Charlotte and Joe, when did you get in?" He asked as he hugged Charlotte and then shook Joe's hand.

James watched this exchanged as Rose walked up behind him. "Mr. Hawk, did my husband rope you into helping with the rest of the decorating?"

"No, I volunteered."

"God Bless him, he still thinks he is thirty years old." She raised her arm motioning towards the coffee stand. "How about a cup of hot coffee to warm you up?"

"Yes, ma'am."

Rose poured him a mug full. "Cream and sugar?"

"Yes please."

Rose poured the items into the steaming cup and handed it to him.

"So, what do you think of our small town?"

"Well to be a little blunt, I wonder if this is all some sort of tourist trap."

"I will admit that it started out like that in order to bring money into the town. Several years ago, the paper mill closed and people were moving away. But it changed into something much more." Rose nodded in the direction of the family in the living room. "That is the Brooks family, Joe is stationed at Fort Detrick. They have been coming here for Christmas every year for about six years now."

"Don't they have their own families to go to?"

27

"Joe's family lives in Florida and Charlotte's family lives in California. We have another couple that comes all the way from London every year."

"Why?"

"Stick around and you'll learn."

"That is what Val says."

Hal walked toward them. "Rosie, I need to go to the hardware store and pick up a few things, do you need anything."

"Yes, I need you to pick up the gift baskets I ordered from the florist and stop by the Memories Diner and pick up lunch. I will call ahead so Val will have it ready for you. What do you want for lunch?"

"I'll take a BLT on wheat with the chips and vanilla panna cotta for dessert. Do you want anything, James?"

"No thank you. Panna cotta I don't know any diners that make panna cotta."

"That is what makes the café so special," Rose answered.

"I will be back in a little bit," Hal headed for the door.

"I better finish putting the mulled wine in the crockpot, so it will be ready for tonight and I have to call the café' Just a thought James, I hear they have some festivals in Chicago too, as a way to make money I mean."

James smiled and Rose triumphantly turned toward the kitchen.

James walked into the living room, sitting down in a chair opposite the family. He pulled his phone from his pocket and saw that he had two messages. The first one was from his boss asking how the next story was progressing. James texted back "going to the first festival this evening."

The second was from his mother informing him she was going to the neighbors for their canasta card game. James texted back, "Have fun." He sipped his coffee and watched the family interact. The kids were excited about the festival and seeing the giant teddy bear.

Rose walked into the living room. "James, I thought you should know there is a fee for the light show tonight."

"How much?"

"Five dollars for adults and two dollars for children. Now before you say gimmick. The money goes to the boys and girls club."

"I wasn't going to say that."

"You were thinking it."

Val stopped her red minivan in her driveway. She bought this log cabin rancher style home two years ago. After she and Maggie spent a year traveling throughout the United States and parts of Europe. It was located on the outskirts of town, about three miles from the diner. Across the street was the neighbor's farm and the backyard butted up to the base of the mountains. She slid out of her seat and then walked toward the side of the van and opened the door, Maggie got out and Val grabbed a few grocery bags from the backseat.

"Come on, little one, we have enough time to change and get ready for the festival."

"Did you turn on the Christmas lights at the diner already?" Maggie asked.

"No, Chris is closing tonight, so he will do that."

She stopped at the front door and unlocked it. "I am going to put these things away," Val said as she and Maggie walked inside. "I am going to get a quick shower. Now you go and change into the outfit I put out for you this morning it's on your bed."

"Are we going to get gyros tonight?"

"Yes, now go."

"I want some soda too," Maggie yelled as she walked down the hallway.

"You'll get hot chocolate or milk instead," Val answered.

After finishing with her shower, Val put on a little make-up, brushed her hair. She walked over to the closet, pulled her black jeans and purple sweater out, and laid them on the bed. She glimpsed over at a picture on her nightstand. She picked up the photo of her and husband Rick standing on the steps of the church on their wedding day, and she felt moisture fill her eyes.

"No tears." She quickly got dressed and then she walked down the hall. She saw Maggie sitting on the couch watching television. Maggie was wearing a red sweater with a polar bear on it and blue jeans with tennis shoes.

"Where are your boots?"

"Do I have to wear them?" Maggie heaved out a dramatic sigh.

"Yes, we are supposed to get more snow. Mush or we are going to be late."

"Oh, all right." Maggie stomped down the hall.

"Rick, she so takes after you," Val whispered

Maggie walked back down the hallway carrying her boots. She sat down on the couch and pulled one on. "The tryouts for the Christmas play are after church tomorrow." She put on her other boot.

"I know. After tryouts we are going to come back here and work on your advent calendar."

"I am going to try out for an angel part this year."

"Good, now let's go" Val held Maggie's coat for her and then she wrapped a red and white scarf around her neck and put a red knit hat on her head and handed her a pair of white mittens.

"Don't forget to turn on the Christmas lights."

"I won't" Val flipped on the light switch for the outside lights. They walked outside. Everything was aglow with white Christmas lights.

Val opened the van door and watched as Maggie climbed into her seat and buckled her seatbelt. Then she climbed into the driver seat.

"Okay kiddo we are off." Val turned on the radio. Rudolph the Red Nosed Reindeer poured out of the speakers. She and Maggie started singing along.

ᏟᎮᎧChapter ThreeᏋᎦᎧ

Val pulled into a parking lot behind the gazebo, she looked up and noticed James Hawk walking toward the gazebo. She noticed he did not have a hat on. *He will be cold before too long.* She got out of the van walked around and opened the door. Maggie slid out of her seat and Val grabbed her hand.

"Okay, we have just enough time to go to the food tent and get some dinner, before the Mayor gives his speech and then turns on the lights."

"Can we get some funnel cake?" Maggie asked.

"Maybe after dinner."

"Okay."

As they entered the food tent, Val noticed that James was standing in line at the fried chicken stand next to Rose and Hal. She looked around the tent and saw a few empty spaces at one of the picnic tables.

"Why don't you go sit down over there." Val pointed to the spaces. "I will get the Gyros and your hot chocolate. Do you want chicken or lamb?"

"Lamb."

"Okay, I will be over there with you in a minute."

James scanned the tent while he was waiting in line. He saw Val and he did a double take. He never noticed how beautiful she was before. Her long hair fell just below her shoulders. And before her slim figure was hidden by her aprons and flannel shirts. He looked back at Rosie.

"I changed my mind. I am going to try the gyros instead."

"They have the best Gyros; I am just in the mood for fried chicken and French fries with gravy," Rose answered.

Val sensed that someone walked up behind her. When she turned, she was startled to find James standing there.

"Good evening," she said.

"Hello, I didn't see your daughter, is she here."

"Yeah she is saving our seats at one of the picnic tables while I get our dinner."

"Gyros instead of hot dogs or hamburgers?"

"She likes lamb and the tzatziki sauce,"

"Tzatziki sauce?"

"It is made with cucumbers, dill, garlic, a little olive oil and yogurt."

Val heard the guy behind the counter say, "next please," and she turned around.

"Two lamb gyros and one hot chocolate and one mulled wine."

"Wine?" James asked.

"Yes, sometimes I have wine and on occasion I make hot chocolate with red wine."

"Well that is different."

"Not where I come from."

Val paid for her order and took the cardboard carrier from the cashier.

"Try the lamb, its good."

"Okay." James turned his attention to the cashier. "I will take one lamb gyro and a mulled wine."

After getting his meal James turned from the stand and scanned the room again. He noticed there was a space between Rose and Val. He ventured over to the table.

"Excuse me." He asked Rose, "Is this seat taken?"

"No, I was saving it for you"

"Where is Hal?" James asked.

"He decided to get a sausage sandwich instead. Every year he has to get his sausage from Mac's stand."

"They are good sausages." Val chimed in. "I get the link sausages we cook at the diner from him."

"There are a lot of people here," James said.

"There will be a lot more later on," Rose answered

Hal walked over and sat down on the other side of Rose.

"That was a long line."

"I am glad you got your sausage sandwich, dear."

"Did the Bakers make it in yet?" Val asked.

"Yes, they made it just in time." She turned to James, "The couple she asked about was the couple from London that I told you about earlier," Rose said.

"Are they staying the whole month again?" Val asked.

"Yes, Charlotte and Joe were so happy to see them, even though they have to leave on Monday. Joe decided to leave the army and take a job in Virginia working for a cybersecurity company. Charlotte is ecstatic that he is getting out of the Army. But they must start packing up their house for their move just after New Year's."

"Why did he get out?" James asked.

"Two tours, one in Iraq and the other in Afghanistan," Rose answered.

"Will they still come here for the lights festival?" Val asked.

"Yes, both the Bakers and Charlotte have made their reservations for next year already."

"Why?" James asked.

"For the families, the Bakers lost their only child to cancer when he was a very young boy. They don't have any grandchildren of their own. They met Charlotte and Joe just before he was leaving for his first tour to Iraq. Charlotte was seven months pregnant with their son and she was very frightened. They just bonded and kept in touch with each other over the years. The Bakers have met several young families and single people here. They consider them to be their adopted children and grandchildren. Everyone has a story or a gift to give."

"Mom."

"Yes, Maggie."

"I finished my Gyro; can I get some funnel cake now?"

"It is almost time for the mayor's speech, so let's get those funnel cakes and head for the gazebo. Okay?"

"Okay."

Val and Maggie got up and gathered their trash.

"Well, have a good evening everyone."

The pair put their trash in the canister and walked over to the funnel cake stand.

"What is her story?" James motioned toward Val.

"That story is only Val's to tell," Hal answered. "So how is your Gyro?

"Good, but your mulled wine is better, Rose."

"You better say that."

James watched Val and Maggie walk out of the tent.

Val and Maggie sat down on the bottom row of the temporary bleachers directly in front of the Mayor's podium. They were lucky to find those seats as the crowd started filing in. Val handed Maggie her funnel cake, then reached around Maggie's neck and straightened her scarf. The high school band marched over to the podium. Once they were on the stand, the bleachers filled in with parents, friends and well-wishers. Val searched the crowd and saw many familiar faces. She noticed Ben, Amy and Chris on the top row of the bleachers. A few moments later she saw Rose, Hal and James sitting at one of the picnic tables at the far end of the bleachers. Soon it was standing room only around the gazebo. The band started playing *Hark the Herald Angels Sing.*

"Mom, can we go see the giant teddy bear."

"Of course, we can."

"That's my favorite."

"Hey, look over there," Val pointed to where Charlotte, Joe, their kids and the Baxter's were sitting. "Do you remember them? Last year they all came over for dinner. You kids all had fun building a snowman in the front yard."

"I think so." They both waved hellos.

The Mayor and his wife plus a few members of the Chamber of Commerce walked up to the gazebo. The mayor stood about six feet tall and had on a black wool coat with matching gloves and a fedora hat. His wife stood about five feet tall and she wore a black fur coat with a matching hat and red gloves. As soon as the music stopped the mayor walked over to his podium.

"Good evening one and all. To those of you who are newcomers to our festival, I am Mayor Rob, and this is my wife Robbie. Our sons could not make it tonight. As some of you know they are attending the University of Maryland and finals are soon approaching." Many in the crowd laughed.

"I won't give a long speech tonight; I know that it is getting a little chilly out here. I would like to thank the members of the Chamber of Commerce and the volunteers who put this Festival of Lights together. I would also like to thank the Festival High School band and the other musicians that will be performing tonight for supporting our festival and of course the Boys and Girls Club. Each year our festival grows in both displays and visitors. The money raised tonight will help fund the new computers for the Boys and Girls Club tutoring program. Of course, the many vendors we have scattered throughout the park grounds would appreciate your support also. I just noticed that the Bakers from London are here, I thought I saw the Millers from New Hampshire somewhere in the crowd." Robbie walked over to her husband and gave a little tug to his coat sleeve.

"That little tug was my wife's signal to end this." The crowd laughed. "So, let us be the first to wish you all a Merry Christmas." The Mayor walked over to the lights on the panel. "I hereby declare the Christmas Lights on Festival to be turned on." He flipped the switch and all the brightly lit displays lit up and the crowd cheered.

"Come on little one, let's head over to the entrance and I will pay our fee."

"Then can we see the Teddy Bear?"

"Okay, and I want to see Santa's bakeshop."

James watched the families mill around the displays and he took some pictures with his camera. He got a shot of Hal and Rose sneaking a little smooch by the giant illuminated snowman. He saw many couples walking arm in arm and kids playing near the displays, laughing and having fun. The giant Teddy Bear caught his attention next. It was made up of some sort of blue material with white lights and big white and brown eyes. He saw Val standing a few feet away from the display. Maggie was giggling and throwing snow up into the air. He reached down for his camera and started to bring it to his face, but something stopped him. Something about Val's expression seemed a little sad. James heard a wandering musician playing music behind him. He turned and watched as the man strolled through the crowd playing *Silent Night* on his guitar. Everything grew strangely quiet as the man walked through the crowd. James took a picture of him and the man nodded his head at James as he went by. James turned his attention back to where Val stood. Maggie was standing beside her and the Bakers were by her side. Mrs. Baker whispered something in Val's ear and hugged her. Val wiped a tear from her face, looked down at Maggie, and smiled.

About an hour and a half later Val tiptoed into Maggie's room. Her baby girl was sleeping soundly. Val pulled the Peanuts gang holiday quilt up to cover her daughter's upper body then leaned over and kissed her forehead. A smile tugged at her lips *Maggie loves Snoopy. I must get her a dancing Snoopy stuffed animal for Christmas this year. Call the toy store on Monday.* With that thought, she shut the door and headed walked toward the living room.

She poured a glass of wine, sat down on the couch, pulled the red quilt around her body, and took a sip of the red wine. She bought that bottle last summer when she took Maggie on vacation to California. Maggie was very bored when they toured the winery, so to compensate Val took her to Disneyland the next day.

Val put down her glass and pulled her laptop off the coffee table. When she turned it on, a picture of her, Rick and Maggie came up on the screen. It was taken at Maggie's christening. *How happy we were then,* Val sighed.

She clicked on the food distributor website and began ordering the supplies she needed for the next week, adding extra supplies for the holiday goodies she would make. It took six months for her to gain a loyal clientele and one Christmas to learn what tourists like. That was a far cry from the crazy turmoil career she had in New York while working as the sous chef at The Purple Bayou Restaurant. A person lived or died there by the number of celebrities, politicians and wealthy clients that were served. Plus, the whims and moods of her boss top chef Elisa Crane. Val still bristled whenever she thought of 'that woman' who had been jealous of her talent. "That was then," Val whispered as she closed her laptop.

James walked into the lobby, set his camera down on the desk and took off his winter coat. He had stayed at the festival for about two hours, taking several pictures of the displays, the visitors, the vendors, and the musicians. He turned as Rose walked into the room carrying a glass of mulled wine.

"James, I was about to send out Hal to look for you. I was wondering if you got lost."

"No, I just stayed and got some interviews for my paper."

"Well, tomorrow we are having a special dinner here and I wanted to make sure that you will be here."

"What time?"

"About five o'clock."

"I will be here."

"Great I hope you like roast duck."

"I have never eaten any."

"Then you are in for a treat. Val is bringing dessert."

"Val and Maggie will be here?"

"Of course." Her expression softened, watching the smile on James' face.

"I better get to work on this story." He ducked his head, feeling a bit awkward at the intensity of her gaze on him.

"Goodnight then." Rose walked toward the living room and James gathered his equipment and headed up the stairway to his room.

Once inside his room, James sat down in the chair next to the window and opened his laptop. He downloaded the pictures from his camera onto his laptop. He scrolled through the photos. They all looked fine to him and he kept scrolling and suddenly stopped when he got to a picture of Amy and Ben standing next to the Santa workshop display. In the background were Val and Maggie with Val pointing to another display. They looked to him like they belonged on a Christmas card. He saved that picture to his personal file and sent several other pictures for his article.

The next morning, Val sat in the last pew of the church watching Maggie on the stage auditioning for the part of an angel in the nativity play. She glanced over as Rose sat down next to her.

"Maggie looks so cute up there. How is she liking school?"

"She loves her teachers and she loves to read."

"Well, that is a good thing. How are you doing?"

"Okay, …Well not really, you know this time of year is hard for me."

"I know, Memories and guilt are tricky things, my dear. I just wish you would stop blaming yourself for what happened. Accidents happen, and life dealt you a raw deal leaving you alone taking care of Maggie."

"I do okay, I have to concentrate on her now."

"But, no one is taking care of you."

Val looked down at her hands for a moment.

"No more lectures then," Rose said. "what type of wine goes with Duck?"

"Pinot Noir or a Merlot."

"Okay, I will see you at five then."

Twenty minutes later Val opened her front door. She and Maggie stomped the snow off their boots before entering the house. Once inside Val hung up their coats and accessories.

"Go change out of your dress, put on the jeans and sweater I laid out for you and I will get lunch ready." Val walked into the kitchen and Maggie following.

"What's for lunch?"

"Chicken soup."

"Becky's mom makes chicken soup from a can."

"Really."

"There is no chicken in it. Only gray squares and noodles."

Val started tickling Maggie and she began giggling.

"Okay noodle, you go change. I have to make an Italian cream cake for dessert tonight."

"Yummy." Maggie smiled and turned away.

"Gray squares and noodles, yuck," Val whispered, watching her daughter skipping down the hall.

Val turned on the kitchen radio and *It's the Most Wonderful Time of the Year* filled the air.

"It will be for Maggie," she whispered.

Rose was wearing a festive Christmas sweater and long black skirt. She walked into the dining room carrying two red poinsettias and placed them on the fireplace hearth. She quickly surveyed the room. The tables were decorated with red tablecloths and silver napkins. The family Christmas china place settings were at the main table and a less expensive Christmas china at the children's table. White candles atop silver candlesticks were on the main dining table and on the fireplace mantle. A large green wreath with a red bow hung above the fireplace. The buffet table had a red tablecloth and a large crystal vase filled with red roses.

"Just enough romance." She spoke out loud.

"Enough romance for who?" Rose jumped and turned at the sound of Hal's voice.

Hal walked over to her and wearing dark blue pants and a tan turtleneck sweater.

"Who are you setting this romantic mood for?"

"For Val and James, mercy knows that girl needs a little romance in her life."

"Why do you say that?"

"It has been three years since Rick died. She has no life outside of Maggie and the diner. That is not healthy."

"Maybe she is still mourning Rick."

"She needs to be shown there is still a chance at a happy life for her."

"Okay, why him?"

"Don't try and tell me you didn't notice the way he looked at her during the lights on festival, and he switched lines after first proclaiming he was hungry for good fried chicken."

"He changed his mind that's all."

"Yeah, keep telling yourself that my dear."

"Well, I will leave the romance plotting up to you."

"I am an expert at it; that is how I landed you. Now I have to go check on the duck and I have a project for you."

"What is that?"

"Please get the board games from the storage room for the kids to play with."

"I expect we will have a rousing game of twister tonight," he said over his shoulder as he walked out of the room.

"I heard that."

Just then James came through the lobby door carrying a few bags from the country store.

"Looks like you have been busy," Hal said as James walked into the room.

"Yeah, I got a few snacks, and a newspaper. Plus, I seem to have lost my gloves, so I got some new ones."

"I have to get some games out of the storage room. Then how about you join me in the den, and we can watch the game. The Ravens are playing the Steelers, so it should be a good match."

"I will bring the snacks than, but where is the television."

"The picture over the fireplace, you flip it and there is a television on the other side."

"Oh, so will Charlotte's husband be joining us?"

"They are spending the afternoon with the Bakers; a local farmer gives sleigh rides this time of year."

"That sounds nice."

"Yeah and of course the farmers need every extra penny they can get this time of year. Well, I better get those games for Rose." He turned and went down the hall as James walked up the stairs.

James put the bags on the bed and pulled his cellphone out of his coat pocket. He noticed he had a voicemail. He tapped the message icon and put the phone to his ear.

"Hi James, this is your mother. All is fine here. Harvey and his nephew came over today and they put the lights up on the outside of the house. The place looks beautiful. I tell you Mrs. Anello must be so jealous. Oh, yeah Jackie at the market says hello. That girl gets prettier every day and she is still single. I saw Josephine when I went to the drug store. She looks like a haggard mess. But that is what she deserves for leaving my son. Harvey invited me over for dinner this evening. Call me later and I loved the article about the festival."

James smiled as he closed the phone. Not that his ex was looking haggard, but at the fact his mother had a high sense of drama. Josephine always wanted a high-cost lifestyle, but she did not want to work for it. A year into the marriage he knew he had made a mistake, but for two years he kept trying to fix things. He left her the day he found out she was having an affair with a local real estate agent. At first, he lived in a small apartment. That was until his father passed away. Then he moved in with his Mom to help her out with the bills and things around the house."

A knock at the door brought him back to reality.

"James, the game is about to start," Hal yelled.

"I'll be right there." James grabbed the bag with the snacks and headed for the door.

Val placed the cake in the travel container and Maggie was sitting at the kitchen table working on their advent calendar.

They had so much fun with that last year she challenged Maggie to come up with a few ideas on her own. There were several strips of paper on the table.

"Did you come up with some more advent ideas for the advent calendar?"

"I still need two more," she answered.

"Let me see what you have here. Making cookies for your teacher Mrs. Jones and giving toys to the poor kids."

"I have a few ideas," she whispered the ideas into Maggie's ear. "What do you think?"

"That will be fun."

"Okay, now go wash your hands."

Maggie walked down the hallway. Val began folding up the pieces of paper and putting them into the wooden advent calendar. Last year she started a new tradition with Maggie, a giving advent calendar. She wrote down several ideas such as giving a stranger a gift certificate to a local gas station, sending cards to soldiers, and baking cookies for a neighbor. She closed the box and put it on the fireplace mantle.

"Maggie, come on, we need to go."

"Mommy, I can't find my mittens."

ᔐᐤ Chapter Four ᔐᐤ

Rose walked into the dining room and surveyed the buffet table. "Duck-check, stuffing–check, corn-check, green beans-check, rolls-check. What am I forgetting?" she whispered to herself "The cranberry sauce." She headed toward the kitchen just as Val and Maggie opened the door to the lobby.

"Hal can you take care of who just walked into the lobby?"

James walked into the lobby just as Val and Maggie were taking off their coats.

"I am afraid Hal is asleep in the living room," James whispered. He took an extra breath when Val turned. She was wearing a long red sweater with black leggings.

"Oh, all right," Val whispered. She reached for the containers she had placed on the chair.

"Here let me help you with those." James volunteered.

"Are the Bakers back yet?"

"Yeah, they are upstairs."

"Maggie, go sit in the living room and I will be there in a minute."

James picked up the large cake container and Val picked up the other smaller boxes.

"I brought extra cookies for the kids and an Italian cream cake."

"That sounds wonderful."

"Who is winning the game?" Val asked as they headed for the dining room.

"The Ravens, do you like football?"

"I am a huge fan, but I don't get a lot of chances to watch the game."

"Why not?"

"With a five-year-old, and a business to run most of my time off is spent watching Disney movies and doing laundry"

Unbeknownst to Val and James, Rose walked into the room carrying the cranberry sauce. She stopped for a moment when she saw the two of them. "Let the magic begin," she whispered.

"James, where is my husband?"

"He is in the living room sleeping."

"Val, there is a cake plate and a silver tray in the kitchen. Can you take care of the desserts while I wake Hal and gather everyone else?"

"Sure." Val walked toward the kitchen.

"Care to help out?" Val asked James.

"Just point me in the right direction."

A few minutes later Charlotte, Joe, their children, the Bakers, Rose, Maggie and Hal trailed into the room.

"Everyone welcome. This is one of many dinners we will have over the holidays. Last year Val had everyone over for dinner and I wanted to host it this time. So, feel free to serve yourselves and then when everyone sits down, we will say grace. Mr. and Mrs. Baker, why don't you start."

The Bakers walked over to the buffet and the rest of the group followed. Val stood in line next to Maggie and James quietly took the place behind the two of them.

"See, they would make a great couple," Rose whispered to Hal.

"I think you are dreaming there, Rosie," he whispered back.

"Just you wait and see."

Val took Maggie's plate. "I will get your plate first and come back for mine."

"Mommy, what's that" Maggie whispered while pointing to the stuffing.

"It is a rice and apple stuffing."

"Rice Stuffing?"

"When people roast duck, they make a rice stuffing, and when people cook turkeys, they make a bread stuffing or sometimes a cornbread stuffing. Trust me you will like it."

"How do you know?"

"It's my recipe." she whispered. "Now go get your drink and remember no eating until grace is said."

"Yes ma'am."

"I am glad your daughter asked the question about the stuffing because I was wondering the same thing," James said.

"How much do you want to bet you will like it?"

49

"If I win you have to pay my entrance fee to one of the festivals."

"Okay, if I win you get to help me put up the display at the diner tomorrow."

"Deal."

Val carried Maggie's plate over to the kid's table and got back in line behind Charlotte.

"We always have to take care of the kids and husbands first, don't we?"

"I only have Maggie, no husband."

"Well, not yet. But he is interested." Charlotte smiled.

Val gave a half-smile back as she took a spoonful of stuffing.

After everyone was seated Val looked over at Maggie and smiled. *Good girl she hasn't touched her food.*

"Care to double our bet," she asked James.

"I am going to play it safe."

Chicken, she thought.

Hal would you please say the blessing," Rose asked. Everyone bowed their heads.

"Dear Lord, thank you for this wonderful feast and please bless the ones that prepared it. Thank you for bringing old friends and new ones to our table this year. Please watch over every one of us and all of those who will travel through here this holiday season. Amen. Now I would like to propose a toast." Everyone lifted their glasses.

"To my beautiful wife and to all of our friends. May this be the best holiday ever." Everyone clinked their glasses.

Val patiently waited for James to take a fork full of stuffing, saw the pleased look on his face as he chewed then swallowed.

"What time do I have to be at the diner tomorrow?" he asked.

"The diner is closed for the day, so why don't you show up at 9:00 a.m."

"Okay."

Val glanced over toward Maggie and noticed how quickly she was finishing her stuffing. She smiled.

"Charlotte, have you found a new house yet?" Rose asked.

"We found a little place to rent for about six months while we look for a more permanent home in northern Virginia."

"When are you officially out of the service Joe?" Val asked.

"January 2nd."

"How did you all find out about Festive?" James asked.

"Well for us, the weather was to blame." Mr. Baxter started.

"Ever since our son died, we've traveled for the holidays. We did not want to stay in such a quiet home when everyone else was celebrating. I guess it was about ten years ago that we decided to tour the East Coast. We spent a week at the Biltmore Estate in North Carolina, and we decided to drive to Vermont for a New England style holiday. We forgot to check the weather forecast and wound up driving into a snowstorm. We saw the sign from the highway and decided to stop. Luckily Rose had a room available. We fell in love with the town and wound up staying for the rest of the holiday."

"Now we come back every year to spend time with our American relatives." Mrs. Baxter added.

"We heard about this town from some friends of ours at the base." Joe started. I knew my unit was going to be called up soon to deploy to Iraq so I convinced Charlotte that we should spend one weekend here before I was scheduled to leave."

"I was sitting in the living room while Joe was helping Hal hang the garland on the porch rails." Charlotte started. "I was so scared about his deployment and tired of trying to be brave. Being seven months pregnant didn't help my emotions much. Elizabeth and Rose walked into the room. The two of them got me laughing and we all have been good friends ever since. We email each other and skype on birthdays and anniversaries. Last year we went to London and stayed for about two weeks. As Elizabeth said, we are family."

"That is amazing," James said.

He looked at Val and nodded as if it was her turn to chime into the conversation. But she only looked at her hands.

"Val, what are your plans for Christmas this year?" Rose asked.

Thank you Rose for getting me out of that one. "Well my mother is staying with my Uncle in Florida during Christmas, but she will be here for New Year's. Once we close the diner on the 23rd and attend the Christmas Eve pageant, Maggie and I will spend a quiet Christmas at home, and since the diner is closed the holiday week. I hope to catch up on some much-needed rest. What about you and Hal?"

"Our kids and grandkids will be arriving on the 23rd and staying until the 27th. What about you, Mr. Hawk?" Rose asked.

"I expect to be spending Christmas with my Mother and a few of our neighbors."

"Well, that sounds nice," Rose added.

"Anyone ready for dessert?" Hal asked.

"Me," Maggie yelled.

Val started to stand up.

"Val you wait on people all week, I got this" Rose said.

"So how many people are checking out tomorrow?" Charlotte asked.

'We have three families checking out tomorrow and three are checking in on Tuesday."

"Will the Martins be checking in?" Val asked.

"Yes, the Andersons and the Collins also. The Martins love the film festival and the downtown open house festival."

Val leaned over toward James "Every year we have a Christmas film festival. Two days of Christmas movies at the theater. They have games and photo booths for the kids," she said.

"What I like are the prices, two dollars a movie," Hal said

"They can't make much of a profit that way," James said.

"That is not the point. They do it to give something nice to the community."

"The downtown open house is on Tuesday night. All of the businesses reveal their Christmas window displays and open up to serve snacks as people go sightseeing through the downtown area."

"Don't forget the Giving Tree," Rose said.

"Every year the Chamber of Commerce has a tree in the lobby filled with cards of the names of families that may need a little extra help with something this Christmas. We call it the Give Back Festival. It is not just toys or gifts they ask for. Some people need help with other things. Last year I got the name of a disabled woman who needed to have someone put up her Christmas tree and other decorations. Then after Christmas I took them down for her." Val said.

"That's nice. Are you going to help her this year?" James asked.

"Unfortunately, no, she had to move into an assisted living facility south of Baltimore."

"Now James, would you like some cake?" Rose asked.

"Of course."

After dinner Val, Rose, and Charlotte started clearing the table. Hal and the rest of the men were in the living room, where Hal was supervising a game of twister with the kids. Val picked up some plates, then paused looking across the opening. She saw James shaking Joe's and Mr. Baxter's hands. *I wonder what that is about.*

Even in the kitchen, Val heard Maggie giggling. "That must be some game of Twister," she said.

"You two leave these dishes and go enjoy some time with your kids. I am going to put some coffee on, and I will join you in a few minutes," Rose said.

54

"Are you sure? That is a lot of dishes." Charlotte answered.

"I have a dishwasher. His name is Hal."

"Okay then." Val said as she headed toward the living room.

"Left foot blue." Val heard Hal say as she and Charlotte walked in the room. Little Maggie was trying to maneuver her left foot to the right spot and down she went. She started laughing, so clearly, she was okay and having fun.

"I think Charlotte, Joe, James, and Val should play a round of twister next," Hal announced.

Val started to protest when Charlotte chimed in before her.

"There is only room for three adult players, so I will sit this round out."

"I will wait and play when my wife does," Joe added.

"I guess that leaves you and me," James said.

Val looked over at Maggie who was sitting next to Hal. Maggie was smiling.

"Okay, one game."

Val and James moved to opposite ends of the twister board.

"Right hand green, Val" Hal started.

A few minutes later both adults were positioned very close to each other on the board. Val's heart started beating a little faster.

"Your perfume smells very nice," James whispered.

"Right foot green, James."

"How am I going to get out of this one and get over to green? Aaagh."

He toppled over taking Val with him. They burst out laughing.

"I think I won." Val laughed harder. James got up and extended his hand. She took hold and he pulled her up. She looked at him and smiled holding his hand one second too long.

"You won Mommy." Maggie's voice brought Val back to Mom reality at that moment.

Rose walked over to James and Val. "Would either of you like a cup of coffee?"

"I would," Val answered.

"Me too."

"Well anyway I think it is Joe and Charlotte's turn next," Hal announced.

"I don't know if I am up to this." Charlotte walked past Val.

"Nothing like a little competition to keep things hopping," Joe answered.

"Maybe Rose and I should play a round."

"In your dreams." Rose handed Val and James the cups of coffee

An hour later Val opened her front door, and then she walked toward the van. She quietly opened the door and unbuckled Maggie's car seat and lifted her out of the van. *She is getting too big for this.* She got through the front door and used her foot to shut it, then carried Maggie into her room. She laid her sleepy child on the bed and pulled off her clothes. Then she eased a snoopy nightshirt over her head. Val drew the bedspread over her child then planted a soft kiss on her forehead.

"Sleep well, my little one."

She closed the door and arched her back. "No rest for the weary."

She walked into the living room, grabbed the Christmas blanket from the back of the couch, sat down and wrapped it around her. She took her laptop off the coffee table and began searching her emails. Nothing from Rick's parents. Weeks earlier she mailed them copies of Maggie's school pictures. Still no reply. *Why do I bother with them?* She answered a few emails from her relatives and paid a few online bills. She yawned as she shut her computer. Lying down on the couch *"I'll lay here for just a few minutes and then get up and start the dishwasher.*

At one o'clock in the morning she rolled off the couch. "Ouch." Weary she walked into the kitchen and turned on the dishwasher. She arched her back and muttered a pain-filled moan. "Great, just great."

Early the next morning Hal walked into the living room and saw Rose sitting on the sofa next to the fireplace. She was blowing into her favorite coffee mug.

"Did Charlotte and Joe get off okay?" he asked.

"Yeah, they checked out about seven. The kids were still sleepy though."

"Well a good time was had by all yesterday."

"Yes, Val and Maggie had a good time and so did James."

"I will concede your point that James and Val seem to be attracted to each other."

"I told you so. She got him to help out with the diner decorations today."

"I wonder what her window theme will be this year."

"Last year she did that Mrs. Claus kitchen and she won 2nd place."

"Yeah, it is hard to beat Betsy's Store. She seemed to corner the market on that first-place ribbon."

"I hope Val wins this time." Rose said with a little bit of sass thrown in.

"Rose, I am surprised at you."

"No, I am just sick of Betsy bragging all the time. Plus, with all Val does for people she deserves a little recognition."

"Val doesn't seem to be the type to seek out recognition."

"Doesn't mean she doesn't deserve some?"

"I know that."

"Well I better get James' and the Bakers' breakfast going."

"While you're doing that, I'll get some firewood."

Just before 9:00 a.m. James parked his rental car in front of the diner. As he got out, he looked across the street and saw Mr. Jeffers picking up a cookie tin from the steps near his doorway. He noticed Mr. Jeffers looking to his left and his right as if searching for who could have left the item there. James closed the car door and walked towards the diner entrance. He tried to pull open the door, but it was locked. He peered through the glass and saw Val talking to a deliveryman. He tapped on the window with his keys. Val jumped and then smiled and waved.

"Don't you move, we need to go over this order." She walked toward the door, reached up, and unlocked the door. She pushed it open just a little and James opened it the rest of the way.

"Good morning," she said.

"Good morning."

"I am sorry, I lost track of time. Do you want a cup of coffee? I just need to settle things with this delivery guy."

"Coffee sounds good."

Val got a mug from under the counter and poured the coffee as James hung up his coat. Val walked over to the delivery guy.

"Now where are my vanilla beans and my Mexican chocolate?"

"Right here ma'am," he replied.

"Do you have the fresh cranberries?"

'Yes, ma'am one case."

"Tell your boss, I need that case of maple syrup he promised me last week."

"Yes ma'am, there was a delay with the delivery from Vermont. It should be here tomorrow. I'll drop it off tomorrow morning."

"Okay, now let me get you a cup of coffee for the road. Do you want cream or sugar?"

"Just sugar, ma'am."

She poured the coffee into a to-go cup and added the sugar. Then she grabbed a bag of cookies from under the shelf.

"Here is a little snack for you to take along."

"Thank you, ma'am," he said as he pushed his dolly towards the front door. Val followed him and locked the door.

"Do you give cookies to all of the delivery drivers?"

"Of course. That way they make sure that I am one of the first stops on their route."

"So, there is a method to your madness."

"Always. Have you had breakfast?"

"Yes. I had breakfast at the Inn."

Val walked over to the stand of delivered items, and she winced when she stretched her back.

James frowned at the look of pain on her face.

"Did you get hurt last night during our game of twister?"

"No, I hurt my back by sleeping too long on an old sofa." She reached for one of the boxes.

James got up. "Here let me help you with those heavy boxes."

"Thank you."

After putting the food away James stretched his back and glanced around the kitchen.

"Where are the decorations for the window?" he asked.

"In my office," She pointed to the door.

James pulled open the door and looked inside. "Well, is there any room for you in this office?"

"We take our window decorations very seriously here in Festive."

"I can see that. Did you unload all of this yourself?"

"Most of it."

"No wonder your back hurts."

"I am a woman with a deadline and a theme."

"What is the theme?"

"Santa's Workshop. Plus, we have to decorate the inside of the diner."

"I should not bet against you ever again."

"That's right."

"Now how about you grab some of those boxes and I will grab my plans, so we can get started."

"Okay,"

Val walked out into the dining area and pulled a long rolled-up sheet of white paper from under the counter. She tucked it up under her arm as she walked toward the jukebox and pushed a few buttons. Johnny Mathis's *Winter Wonderland* filled the air.

"Why do you need laminated flooring?" James asked as he walked into the room.

"Santa's Workshop has to have a floor."

"And the bookshelves?"

"Come here, I will show you my plans" She unrolled the paper as James walked over to the table.

"Wow, those look like an architect's drawing. Did you do those?"

Val hesitated for a moment trying to compose her face. "Yeah, my husband was an architect. But he died a few years ago so, it's just me and Maggie now."

"I'm sorry. I didn't mean to pry."

"You could not have known. So, Santa's Workshop." She tried to change the subject.

"Well it is a good thing you have a huge window."

"This place had several incarnations before I took over. I think at one time it was a lady's dress shop. Now back to work. On one wall there will be a stack of presents and a ladder. On top of the ladder will be an elf doll with another gift in his hand. On the other wall there will be bookshelves filled with toys and art supplies. I have a few tables and chairs to go in the middle space."

"What will be on the tables?"

"There will be elf dolls working on various projects plus various gift boxes that the elves will be filling with their gifts. Then there is the screen that Chris made. He painted it, complete with Santa looking over his naughty and nice list."

"How are you going to attach the screen?"

"It is on a folding wooden frame, sort of like a dressing screen. There are rings that Chris screwed into the frame so that we can hook onto the walls, so it doesn't fall down."

"Where did you get all of the toys and supplies from?"

"This also at one time used to be an antique shop, so I found some of them. The Mayor had a collection of antique toys and he lent me a few. Plus, my Mom sent me some unique items that were her parents' toys."

"I'm going to be here for a while huh."

"I will make you a wonderful lunch. First, we must hang the curtains. The Curtains for the big reveal."

"What?" James asked.

"The crowds and judges go to each business and we have our reveal. Prizes are awarded at the end of the night. Last year I got second place."

"What does the winner get?"

"A blue ribbon."

"And?"

"A basket filled with donated prizes from the other businesses."

"And?"

"Okay, bragging rights."

"I knew it."

"So, sue me, I am a little competitive."

"A little."

"Would you go get the rest of the boxes please, and I will start putting up the curtains."

"Okay,"

James walked into the office and grabbed a few boxes. When he turned back toward the door and he noticed a wedding photo on Val's desk.

"That guy looks familiar," he whispered.

He sat the boxes down on the floor, took a picture of the photo with his cellphone, and sent it to his boss.

Back in the other room James saw Val standing on a small stepladder pushing the red curtains across the gold curtain rod. He put the boxes down on the table and felt his phone begin to vibrate. The message read, "That photo is Rich Young. His parents own the Window Garden Hotel chain. He died a few years back in a car accident. The woman in the picture was his wife Valerie and I think they had a kid. She was a chef at one of those swanky hotels in New York. Why do you ask? And the article you sent about the Bakers will be in tomorrow's edition." He stared at his phone for a moment.

Val snapped her fingers to get his attention. "Hey, earth to James."

"I'm sorry, what did you need."

"I asked you to hand me the other curtain."

"Sure."

"You were really into reading what was on your phone."

"Just a message from my boss."

"James."

"Yes."

"The curtain."

"Oh, yeah."

He put the phone back in his pocket, walked over to the table, grabbed the red material, and handed it to her.

"You still have a job, right?"

"Yeah."

"So, smile and please put some Christmas tunes on the jukebox. We got a workshop to create."

He punched in a few buttons on the jukebox and Doris Day came over the speakers.

"I feel like the Grinch," he whispered.

After they finished putting down the flooring Val stood up and tried to stretch.

"Ouch, time for some Advil and a coffee break."

"How about I get the coffee?"

"Being served in my own restaurant, I could get used to that."

They walked over to the counter and Val got a bottle out of her bag as James poured the coffee. He put cream and sugar in hers.

"How did you know I like cream and sugar?"

"I am observant."

That's interesting."

"Where is Maggie?"

Back in school. Thanksgiving break is over, and she is counting the days until Christmas break."

"We did the same thing as kids, right?"

"Right."

"By the way did you notice someone left a cookie tin on Mr. Jeffers's doorstep today?"

"You don't say. Must be the town elves"

"You are not going to try to convince me the town has elves around here are you?

"Christmas elves come in all shapes and sizes."

⟨♪Chapter Five⟩

Two hours later Val and James took a step back from the window and glanced around the scene. Val smiled.

"Are we good?" James asked.

"Yes, the only things we have left to do is put the screen up and decorate the inside of the diner. But first, how about some lunch?"

"That sounds good."

"How about a hamburger and a salad?"

"Great."

"Is iced tea all right?"

"Yes."

"Grab a seat at the counter and I will get lunch started"

Val disappeared into the back room while James sat down in his usual spot at the counter. He pulled his smartphone out of his pocket and brought up Google. He punched in Rich Young's name and opened the article about the accident. His eyes quickly scanned the article.

"Richard John Young died on December 15th, 2013 from injuries received in a single car accident believed caused by him driving fast on black ice; he was not wearing a seatbelt. Mr. Young was the heir apparent to the Window Garden Hotel chain, and his younger sister will probably inherit the fortune now."

James heard the kitchen door swing open and he put his phone in his pocket.

"Here is your tea and salad. I put Catalina dressing on your salad."

"You remembered."

"Only a few of us around here like Catalina salad dressing. Now how do you want your hamburger?"

"Well done."

"Okay, I'll be right back." She went back toward the kitchen.

As the door closed behind her James pulled his phone back out of his pocket.

The article went on to say that Val was the sous chef at the Purple Bayou Restaurant. There was a picture of her carrying Maggie out of the funeral home. Another picture showed Richard's parents. They appeared to be very prim and proper he thought. Cold-hearted almost. James' eyes went back to the picture of Val. She had on a blue coat and her face was puffy from crying.

"James," Val yelled from the kitchen. "Do you want lettuce and tomato on your burger?"

"Just lettuce" he yelled back and turned off his phone.

Val walked out of the kitchen carrying his burger and salad on a large platter and only a small salad for hers.

"What, no burger?"

"Tonight, is Monday, and Maggie gets to pick what she wants for dinner and it is usually one of three things. Mac and Cheese, hamburgers or pizza. So, I tend to eat a light lunch on Mondays."

James took a bite of his burger. "That is perfect. Where did you learn to cook?"

"Mom taught me, using her handed-down recipes."

"I think there is much more to that story. I have noticed how you watch people while they eat. To check if they are enjoying themselves. I am pretty sure that was your duck recipe along with stuffing recipe we had yesterday."

"I attended a culinary school in Baltimore. And after my husband died, I traveled a bit and learned how to prepare different cuisines."

"Did you visit Festive when you lived in Baltimore?"

"No, I heard about it, but I did not visit here. Now stop stalling with all the questions, we still have the tree to put up and the screen too."

"Okay, can we stop with the Christmas music for a little while though?"

Val walked over to the jukebox and punched in a few numbers. *Smells Like A Teen Spirit* started playing.

"I should have kept my mouth shut."

"Yep."

A few minutes after 3:00 p.m., Val pulled her coat down from the wall hook and put it on.

"I'll be right back; I have to meet Maggie's school bus." She pulled her keys from her pocket and locked the door once she was on the other side. Turning to the right she disappeared from his view.

"This place looks like a diner in Santa's Village." James said as he pulled out his phone and took a few pictures. On every table she had placed a black metal lantern with a winter scene inside. One had a toy truck with a Christmas tree in its bed and snow. There was another one with a white church inside, and others where filled with snowmen or animals. The tree was decorated with red and silver ornaments and the jukebox was outlined with red garland. Even the old metal cash register had Christmas magnets on it.

A few minutes later, Val opened the front door and Maggie ran inside.

"Hi," she said.

"Hi Maggie, is it snowing again."

"Yes," Maggie brushed some snowflakes off her jacket sleeve. "Guess what."

"What?"

"I am going to be an angel in the Christmas play."

"Really, wow that is exciting."

"Yeah, I am angel number four, we get to sing and be on the stage."

"Maggie, do you like the decorations?" Val asked.

"I think it's pretty. But where is Grandpa's train?"

"I think we will put that up at our house this year."

"Okay."

"You have a seat, while Mr. James and I load up some of these boxes in the van, okay?"

"Yes, ma'am."

No peeking into the front window, Santa and his elves are watching."

I can set up my camera phone to watch her also," James volunteered.

I promise, I will be good," Maggie said while she sat down at the counter.

"I don't know, you may be tempted," James said. "What do you think?" he asked Val.

We can trust her."

Okay then."

We will be right back," Val said and grabbed a few boxes, while James grabbed the rest, and they headed for the back door.

How long before temptation gets the best of her," he asked as Val unlocked the back door.

Move quickly."

At 4:00 p.m. James pulled into the hotel parking lot. His phone started vibrating. He swiped the screen with his hand and saw the message.

"What's up with wanting information on Rich Young? Did you have a story there or not?"

James texted back "Not sure yet." He put his phone in his coat pocket and got out of the car.

Rose was carrying a plate of cookies from the kitchen to the lobby area when James walked through the door.

"Good afternoon, James, did you enjoy your day helping Val?"

"Yes, I did," James said and took off his coat. "She did an amazing job with the window display."

"Would you like a cookie?"

"No thank you."

Rose put the tray on the lobby table next to a crock-pot. From the smell in the room James could tell she made another batch of mulled wine.

"Well, I hope she wins this year. It would be nice to take Betsy down a peg or two."

"Does she get carried away with the bragging rights?"

"She put all of her blue ribbons in shadow boxes and has them displayed on the wall behind the counter. Plus, she has a blue-ribbon image on all of the flyers she gives out with the tag line Five-Year Christmas Window Champion."

"I have to admit it was a little eerie driving through town and seeing curtains covering up all of the shop windows. Like the whole place shut down."

"Tomorrow night it will be crazy busy, I am sure Val will be giving out free cookies and Mexican hot chocolate."

What is Mexican hot chocolate?"

"Hot chocolate with a little cinnamon and cayenne pepper in it."

"Sounds different."

"Last year it was the hit of the evening."

"I heard her talking to the delivery guy about Mexican chocolate, so I can almost guarantee she will be serving it tomorrow."

"Where is Hal this evening?"

"He is doing some Christmas shopping."

"Is there another restaurant in town? Since the diner is closed today, I have to find another place."

"If you go past the park about a half a mile there is an Irish pub and they serve dinner also."

"Thank you."

"Would you like a glass of mulled wine?"

"Maybe later."

James grabbed his coat and walked up the stairs toward his room.

Once inside the door James tossed his coat on the bed and got his laptop out from its case. He sat down by the window and turned it on. For a moment he hesitated, but then shook his head, clearing the cobweb of other thoughts and typed Val's name in the search box. He found one article concerning a court case. He clicked on the subject line. The article was about a custody case concerning Maggie and Rich's parents trying to get custody of their granddaughter. They claimed Val was a neglectful parent because she put her career above her daughter. There was a direct quote from Mr. Young where he said, "If Val had been home taking care of Maggie, instead of trying to impress other cooks, my son would not have died that day."

"That is harsh," James spoke out loud.

He started reading the article again, reporting that Val won custody once the contents of Rich's will were presented as evidence in the case. The reporter wrote that it was Rich's expressed wish that his parents never be allowed to raise Maggie.

"I wonder what happened there," James said. "He must have really hated them."

James closed his laptop and grabbed his coat.

"I need a beer."

Hal walked into the lobby as James was walking out the door. Hal had several shopping bags and James could see there were toys sticking out the top of a couple of them.

"Hello, James,"

"Hello, Hal,"

"I see you have been Christmas shopping."

"I got a gift for Rosie and some toys for the Give Back festival."

"The Give Back Festival?"

"Yeah, that is a festival where everyone chooses to help out those who are less fortunate. They have a bin for people to put toys in just in case extras are needed. Every year Rosie and I get toys for the kids."

"What happens to the extra toys if they are not needed?"

"They are donated to the children's wing at the hospital. Where are you headed?"

"The Irish pub."

"They make a great corned beef sandwich and the Guinness is good too."

"I'll keep that in mind."

"Oh yeah, snow is coming down pretty thick now and we are supposed to get a few more inches before morning."

"Thanks for letting me know." James walked outside.

Rose walked into the room as James closed the door.

"So how did their day go?"

"He spent all day with Val."

"Is that a good thing? I mean he is a reporter."

"Hopefully he isn't all work and no play." A teasing smile touched her lips.

"Rose! I am shocked you would say such a thing."

"No, you're not." Her smile grew bigger. "Now did you get the football and Bratz dolls like I asked you too."

"Yes, plus I got a few toy trucks and a stuffed animal bear."

"What about the board games?"

"I got Clue, Trouble, Connect Four, and Hungry Hungry Hippos."

"I guess that is enough."

"For now."

"What does that mean?"

"I am sure you will send me out for more toys tomorrow."

"That is my job."

"Is Val having her party this year?"

"She hasn't said. I'm sure she will do something for her staff."

"I hope she invites us again."

"You just want to eat crown roast again."

"Yes, ma'am and plum pudding."

"What did you get for me?"

"A lump of coal."

"Really?"

"Make that two lumps of coal."

"You just might wind up in the doghouse this Christmas."

"Since we don't have a dog that may be interesting."

"Go get a cookie and a cup of wine."

"Yes, ma'am."

"We are having leftovers for dinner and it should be ready in about a half-hour. In the meantime, please call Billy and see if he can shovel the sidewalk tomorrow before school."

"I can do it," he said from the doorway.

"I am not making any emergency trips to the hospital this year," she called out. "did you forget what happened last year when you fell and sprained your ankle and your wrist? You missed a bunch of the festivals. Call Billy or I am going to put a dozen pieces of coal in your stocking this year."

"All right."

James parked his car in front of Delaney's Irish Pub. The wooden building looked more like it belonged in the west than in a small town in Maryland. He opened his car door and the wind and snow forced him to pull the neck of his coat a little closer as he headed across the parking lot.

He opened the heavy wooden door, shut it behind him and walked toward the bar. He was impressed by the beautiful carvings on the front of the bar. He took a long look around, then noticed Ben seated at one of the tables talking to the Mayor.

"Hey James, come over here."

"Hi, Ben."

"James, this is Mayor Robert Kaiser."

"Good evening, Mayor" James reached and shook his hand.

"Sit down and join us."

"Okay, what is good here?" James took a seat at the round table.

"The corned beef and the fish and chips." The Mayor said.

"The Guinness is great, but I can't have any since I may be driving the plows tomorrow if this snow gets very thick," Ben said.

"Will the festival be canceled if the snow is too heavy?"

"No, it is supposed to end by early morning," answered the Mayor.

"Schools may be delayed for a little while," Ben added

"James, what do you do for a living?"

"I am a reporter for the Chicago Telegraph Newspaper."

"You're the one who wrote the article on the Lights on Festival." the Mayor said.

"Yes, I am. How did you know about that?"

"My cousin lives in Chicago. It was a nice article."

"Thank you."

The waitress walked over to the table. She had a green elf hat on her head. "What can I get for you this evening?" She looked at the mayor first.

"I'll have the cottage pie and an Irish coffee."

"I'll have the fish and chips and an iced tea," Ben added.

"I'll have the corned beef sandwich with chips and a Guinness."

"Thank you gentlemen and I'll get your drinks right away."

"Mr. Mayor, why did the town start to have all of these festivals?"

"There used to be a paper mill on the outskirts of town, when they closed the mill a lot of the people lost their jobs, some of them lost their homes. The town lost its hope and some buildings became rundown. Before long, it was as if the entire town was in some sort of depression. We needed a way to attract tourism to the town and to provide hope again."

"This was a way to raise money?" James asked.

"Yes, it started that way. But what happened, the town was coming together and having pride in the community again—neighbors helping each other. Families came together and people here have friends all over the world. It's a place where both residents and strangers are part of a family for some people and for others it is a place to rest and regroup. We are a part of the international tourism community. It has taken a while, but business outsiders are really taking notice of our town."

"What do you mean by outsiders?"

"The Maryland State University is going to build a branch here in the spring. There is a cabinet making company that is going to take over where the old paper mill was. That is still in negotiations, but I should be able to announce the final plans sometime in January. Another company is going to build a ski resort about five miles from town."

"I am really looking forward to the ski resort being built," Ben added.

"Why, do you ski?"

"No, but they will need maintenance men and construction workers."

"Have you lived here all your life?"

"Yeah, well sort of."

"Sort of?"

"When my Dad couldn't find work and things got tough," Ben added. "We moved to Baltimore for a year."

"Why did you leave Baltimore?"

"My parents hated it there. We are small-town people. The City was not the right fit for us. Dad worked several jobs to keep a roof over our heads and food on the table. When my Grandparents passed on, they willed my parents their house. So, my parents sold it and my father opened the hardware store. They had their struggles for a few years, but things are easier now."

"Will you run the hardware store someday?"

"No, that job will go to my brother. I want to start a landscaping and construction business."

The waitress brought their drinks over. "Here you go, your food will be out in a few minutes."

"Do you mind if I write about the things, we talked about this evening in one of my stories?"

"I don't mind, but don't bring up anything about the cabinet company since we are still working on finalizing that deal."

"Ben?"

"I would have to ask my parents; I am not sure how my Dad would feel about having a lot of people know how much he struggled."

"Okay."

"I can let you know tomorrow night."

"That will be fine."

Val flipped over a grilled cheese sandwich, let that side brown, and then slid it onto a plate. She got two bowls out of the cabinet and filled them with tomato soup. She put the food on the table and stretched her back. Maggie was sitting in the living room coloring a picture from her Christmas coloring book.

"Mom, can I put a picture in the Christmas card we are sending to the fire station?"

"That would be a great idea. Dinner is ready, go wash your hands."

Maggie scampered off towards the bathroom.

"Okay, Val whispered to her aching back "I am a woman on a cookie baking mission, so lighten up on the pain."

"Mommy," Maggie spoke as she came back. She pulled out her chair and sat down. "What type of cookies are you making for tomorrow?"

"Almond cookies and Thumbprint cookies filled with Christmas jam."

"Christmas jam, what's that?"

Val sat down next to her daughter. "Remember I made jam a couple of weeks ago, with strawberries and cranberries in it."

"Oh, so that is Christmas jam."

"Yes, ma'am." She watched her daughter begin eating, and then she started eating her own supper.

"You have play practice tomorrow after school," she reminded Maggie. "Then Chris is going to pick you up and bring you back to the diner to hang around until the festival starts. Then you can stay with me at the diner or walk around the festival with Amy and Ben."

"I hope we don't have school tomorrow."

"Sorry little one the snow is supposed to stop by morning. There may be a delay, but I doubt that you will miss a whole day of school."

"Rats." She took another bite of her sandwich. "You make the best grilled cheese sandwiches."

"Tell me something you learned today in school."

"Babar the elephant likes to ride in the elevator."

"Yes, he does and what else."

"We played with a giant parachute in gym class."

"Did you like that?"

"It was okay, at recess we had to stay inside, so Jenny and I played house."

"What about math class?"

"Four quarters make one dollar."

"That's right."

Maggie put down her sandwich and looked sadly at her plate for a moment.

"Why the sad face?"

"Did my Daddy like Christmas?"

Val swallowed hard. "Yes, he did."

"Before he went to heaven, did we get to spend a Christmas together?"

"Yes, you had your very first Christmas together. Your Dad read to you *Twas the Night Before Christmas*, and I read to you the Christmas story about baby Jesus."

"Did I like it?"

"It was kind of hard to tell, you fell asleep. Now the next day you were the hit of the Christmas Celebration. You had on a red velvet dress with candy cane tights and you laughed and giggled. Especially when your Dad tried to sing the Mr. Grinch song. You laughed at him, and you made everyone else laugh."

"I wish I had a Daddy."

Val felt a tear run down her face. She quickly brushed it away.

"I know honey bunny, but we are going to make great Christmas holidays. Later this week we will go to the movies, the outdoor skating rink opens next week, and Santa will be at the reindeer games. What do you want for Christmas? You better work on your letter tonight, so I can mail it for you tomorrow."

"Can I do it now?"

"Finish your dinner first."

After dinner Val started baking the thumbprint cookies while Maggie was sitting at the coffee table working on her Christmas list. Thank goodness I have this to do tonight. She blinked back another tear as she wiped her flour-covered hands on her apron.

"Mommy, how do you spell puppy?"

"Back to reality," Val whispered.

♟Chapter Six♞

J ames opened the pub door to leave and he immediately saw that the snow was getting heavy and thick. He gathered his coat around his neck and headed toward the car. Luckily the rental agency had put an ice scraper in the trunk. After he finished scraping off the windows he got in the car, and he felt his phone vibrating in his coat pocket. He pulled it out to look at the screen and noticed he had a voicemail message. He thumbed the button.

"Hello James, this is your mother. Is this thing working? Anyway, I am just wondering how you are doing? Are you eating right? Do you need anything? I bet you lost your gloves again. Do you need me to send you more gloves? Harvey and I went Christmas shopping today. I bought a train set for one of the kids from church. Harvey took me to Barb's Tea Room for lunch and I bought some of her Christmas tea blend. It is wonderful. I can't wait 'til you come home. Your cousin Katherine says hello, I ran into her at the liquor store. I've got to have bourbon to make my eggnog recipe. Well, call me soon. I worry about you."

James laughed "Ma your eggnog recipe could knock over a horse," he whispered as he put the key in the ignition and started the car. *"Have Yourself a Merry Little Christmas"* came on the radio. He started singing along with Bing Crosby as he drove away.

Rose and Hal were sitting in the living room when James walked into the Inn. They had a fire going in the fireplace. Hal had a piece of paper in one hand and pen in the other. James walked toward the fireplace to warm himself.

"Good evening, you two."

"Good evening, James, did you go to the pub for dinner?" Rose asked.

"Yes, the food was great, and I had dinner with Ben and the Mayor."

"I expect Ben will be busy clearing the streets," Hal added.

"Yeah, he mentioned something about that."

"The Mayor and I talked for a while about the festivals."

"Our Mayor can talk the ear off a camel," Hal said.

"I agree, so what are you doing this evening?'

"We are making a list of supplies and groceries we need. Plus, the rest of the Christmas chores we need to do before the big day. That reminds me, I need you to pick up some magazines and children's books also. Carrie's father is back in the hospital again, I am sure she would enjoy having something to read and some things for the kids to do."

"Who is Carrie?" James asked.

"She is a teller at the bank. Her father has pneumonia and dementia, so she has a rough go of it. Her husband is stationed in Japan. She had to stay to help out with her father."

"That must be hard." James reached into his pocket and pulled out a hundred-dollar bill.

"Here give this to them also, maybe they need help with food or Christmas presents." He handed the money to Hal.

"Thank you, James. I know they will appreciate it."

"I better go work on my story, Goodnight."

"Goodnight."

James headed toward his room. Rose waited for him to leave.

"Seems like James is starting to catch on about what makes this place so special," Rose said.

"Maybe, he is. I am looking forward to tomorrow night's festival. Especially all of the snacks and treats we get to nibble on while walking around and looking at all the displays." Hal added.

"Tomorrow morning there is a meeting at the diner for the Chamber of Commerce Board members."

"Does Val know?" Hal asked.

"I better call and remind her just in case. Plus, I want to order one of her butterscotch pies for next week. Did you talk to Mr. Robertson about the reindeer petting zoo?"

"Yes, he is bringing four reindeer to the festival and he agreed to play Santa Claus this year too."

"The kids will love it."

"So will I."

"You are a big kid."

"Where are the Bakers this evening?"

"They went out to dinner and came back early"

"I forgot to ask; did all of the other guests get in okay?"

"Everyone is here."

"I am going to get another log for the fire, I put some extra logs on the porch this afternoon just in case we got more snow than the weatherman predicted."

"Good thinking my dear. Now I better call Val. would you like a cup of hot tea?"

"Yes, thank you."

Rose put the kettle on the stove, picked up the phone, and punched in Val's number.

"Hello?"

"Hi, Val. This is Rose."

"Hi Rose, how are you?"

"Fine dear and you?"

"Sore and tired."

"Sore?"

"I hurt my back the other night and Advil is not helping. However, I am determined to finish baking the cookies for the festival tomorrow night."

"I was just calling to remind you that the Chamber of Commerce board will be meeting at the diner for our annual Christmas breakfast."

"I will be making the cinnamon rolls tomorrow morning. I know how much the board likes them. I ordered a special blend of Christmas tea and Chris is coming in for a little while to help out."

"Did you hear about Carrie?"

"Yes, I am making an extra batch of cookies for her and the boys."

"James donated a hundred dollars to help them out."

"Really?"

"I think our small-town spirit is growing on him."

"Maybe."

"I need to order a butterscotch pie for Saturday night. We are having a dessert buffet here after dinner. I am making sugar cookies, pumpkin pie, and chocolate cake. Plus, your pie."

"How many people will be there?"

"Whoever shows up. Will you and Maggie be able to come?"

"Maybe. How about I add some Mexican wedding cakes and some Madeleine cookies."

"I was hoping you would say that."

"Okay, thanks, I better get my next batch of cookies out of the oven."

"Goodnight then."

"Goodnight," Val said.

Rose poured the hot water into the teapot and put in the tea bags. Hal walked into the kitchen.

"I was wondering what was taking so long."

"I was talking to Val. She is going to make some extra desserts for Saturday night."

"That is good. Did she remember about the meeting?"

"Yeah, she has that covered. I am worried about her though, she hurt her back really bad."

"Being on her feet all day tomorrow and for the festival won't help."

"No, it won't. She will need someone to help her tomorrow night." Rose drifted off into a mental space.

"Rosie, Rosie."

"What?"

"You drifted off somewhere."

She turned and got the mugs from the cabinet and poured the tea into the cups.

"I was just thinking about who we could get to help Val out tomorrow night."

"You are playing matchmaker again."

"Maybe I am."

"Yes, you are. But I will just say this once. He is from Chicago and a reporter. Val left the big city behind for some peace in her life."

"Locations can always change, my dear, if someone really loves someone else."

"I just hope Val doesn't get her heart broken."

"I know what I am doing. After all, didn't I get Ben and Amy together?"

"Yes."

"And the Mayor and his wife?"

"Yes"

"Then hush up and drink your tea."

"Anything you say, dear."

Val put the lid on the last tin of cookies, and she looked over at Maggie who gave out a huge yawn. Val smiled as she walked over to the coffee table.

"Time for bed little one."

"Do you really think I will have school tomorrow?"

"Yes, I will check on-line early tomorrow just in case. Now put your coloring book away and hand me the list for Santa."

"Let's see here, Twister, Barbie dream house, Barbie car, Barbie clothes, Barbie and Skipper dolls, dancing Snoopy, Babar books, tea set, Connect Four, and a puppy. I will mail that tomorrow along with the card for the firefighters."

"Did Mr. Jeffers get his cookies?"

"Yes."

"I like being a secret elf."

"I thought so, now march to the bathroom little one."

"Okay." She moaned and shrugged at the same time.

About half an hour later Val was sitting on Maggie's bed. Maggie was kneeling beside it.

"Now what about your prayers?"

"Now I lay me down to sleep. I pray the Lord my soul to keep, if I die before I wake, I pray the Lord my soul to take. God bless Mommy, Amy, Ben, Chris, Angie, Debbie, Mr. Jeffers, my teachers, My Grandma and my Daddy in heaven. Plus, the new puppy I will get for Christmas, I hope. Amen."

"Amen. Now in bed."

Maggie climbed in underneath her covers.

"Goodnight," Val kissed her daughter on the forehead. "I love you."

"I love you, Mommy."

In the living room Val gathered up the Christmas card, and Maggie's Christmas list then slumped onto the couch and started crying.

"I shouldn't have to tell my child that her Dad loved Christmas and her God. He should be here helping me tuck her in at night. Giving her butterfly kisses. Okay, no more tears. I don't have time to feel sorry for myself."

Val walked to the kitchen and started putting the dishes in the dishwasher. She looked at the clock above the sink. Great, I still have a load of clothes to do. No rest for the exhausted and downhearted.

A little after midnight Val went into her bedroom and pulled back the sheets. She knelt by her bed.

"Dear God, Thank you for your many blessings. Please watch over my daughter and bless her with a sound mind and a giving heart. Please watch over my loved ones, employees, and keep them safe. Please give me the strength to make it through each day. May I remember there are those who are far worse off than me and please bless them with whatever they need. Amen."

At 1:00 a.m. James finished typing his notes from his conversation with the Mayor into his computer. He picked up his cellphone from the bed and checked it for messages. One text came from his boss.

It read "Any news about Val Young? I emailed you an article about her being a guest chef on one of those cable channel cooking contests shows. Let me know."

James opened his email and quickly scanned the article. Val was in a Christmas baking contest. He noticed the date of the article was three days before Rich's accident. There was a picture of Val standing next to a gingerbread castle, with miniature reindeer and elves standing outside the castle. The article said they were made from fondant.

"She won first place." He said out loud.

He picked up his phone and texted his boss "Not much of a story, she just runs a diner now."

He was about to close his phone.

"I forgot Ma." He then texted his mother.

"Hi Mom, I am glad you had a good day. Everything is fine here. I'll call soon.

He shut off his phone and headed for the shower.

6:00 a.m. Chris and Amy walked into the diner. Val was standing at the counter pouring herself a cup of coffee.

"I hate snow," Chris said as he hung up his coat.

"You're living in northern Maryland; you better get used to it. Ben has been out plowing the roads since four this morning, so you know he will be tired." Amy answered as she put her gloves in her coat pocket.

"Speaking of tired." Chris motioning toward Val just as she yawned.

"Good morning you two. I had maybe fifteen minutes of sleep last night. At least it seems that way. Plus, my daughter is so excited that she got a two-hour delay. She is sleeping in my office. My back hurts. Basically, a tractor-trailer has run over me so to speak. Before I forget, the Chamber of Commerce board is coming in and I have to make cinnamon rolls." Val yawned again.

"Boss," Chris started. "I am going to put some salt down on the sidewalk. Amy and I will set up everything while you take care of the cinnamon rolls."

"Deal and thank you."

Val grabbed her purse from under the counter, walked into the bathroom, and turned on the cold water. She splashed cold water on her face. After drying off she looked in the mirror.

"Wow, this can't be right. I don't look like that person." She pulled her hair back into a ponytail. She searched for her eye drops. "They have got to be in here." Her fingertips felt the familiar bottle. "Got it." She put drops in both eyes. She then pulled her make-up bag out of her purse. "Okay, Avon moisturizer do your stuff."

Chris walked through the front door carrying the bag of salt. Amy was setting up the tables with the sugar, salt and pepper containers. Chris walked towards her.

"Since the diner is closing tonight for the festival, how about I take the afternoon shift and we send the boss home."

"What are the specials today?" Amy asked.

"Lasagna with tossed salad and garlic bread, Roasted pork with potato gnocchi and tomato sauce. Do you know how to make those?"

"No."

"Hopefully after the lunch crowd she can get a few minutes of sleep in the office."

A few minutes past 8:30 a.m. Mr. Jeffers walked into the diner. He hung his coat on the rack and stomped the snow off his boots.

"Good morning Mr. Jeffers," Chris said.

"Morning, what are you doing here? Don't you work the evening shift?"

"Yes, Val needs the extra help. The Chamber is having their breakfast meeting here today."

"Well, they need to do something about parking around here."

"I agree with you there," Amy said as she handed Mr. Jeffers a cup of coffee.

"Do you want your usual today?"

"Of course, where's Val?"

"In the back finishing up some cinnamon rolls for the board members."

Maggie pushed open the door to the kitchen and immediately took the seat next to Mr. Jeffers.

"Good morning, Mr. Jeffers."

"Good morning, Maggie. Why are you here? Don't you have school?"

"The schools are opening late today due to the snow," Amy answered.

"Oh."

"I am going to be an angel in the Christmas Eve play."

"That's nice."

"Mommy mailed my letter to Santa this morning."

James parked his car across the street from the dinner. He noticed some of the shopkeepers were pouring salt on the sidewalks. He stomped his feet on the sidewalk as he opened the diner's front door.

"Good Morning everyone," he said as he sat down next to Maggie.

"Good Morning, James," Amy answered. "What can I get for you this morning?"

"How about a cup of coffee and I'll have scrambled eggs with bacon and toast."

Val walked out the kitchen door carrying Maggie's breakfast and immediately locked eyes with James.

He's here and I look like something a train hit. Great, just great. Smile and fake it.

"Good morning everyone." She put a plate of scrambled eggs and bacon in front of Maggie.

"Mom, can I have a cinnamon roll now?"

"After you finish your breakfast. Now orange juice or apple?"

"Orange juice, please."

"Val, are you all right?" Mr. Jeffers asked.

"Well... I will be. Now I will get the oatmeal going and James' order. Everything will be out in just a few minutes."

James stared at Val as she walked towards the kitchen and Chris was watching him.

"Here's your coffee."

"Thank you, Chris."

"Val has been like a sister to me and you should remember that."

"I will."

A few minutes later Val came into the dining area carrying both Mr. Jeffers' and James' breakfast.

"There you go gentleman." She put the plates down on the counter in front of them. Then she looked over at Maggie's plate and noticed it was empty.

"Good job. I owe you one cinnamon roll."

"Mom, cut it in half please."

"Okay," Val headed for the kitchen.

"I asked Santa for a puppy," Maggie announced.

"That's a pretty big gift, do you think you're old enough to take care of a puppy?" Amy asked.

"I'm almost six."

Val put the cinnamon roll down in front of her daughter. Maggie looked at it for a moment.

"Mr. Jeffers would you like a piece?"

"Maggie, I don't know if I should."

"Try it, you may like it," Amy said.

Val pulled a saucer out from under the counter and put the half on it. She smiled at Maggie as she gave the piece to Mr. Jeffers.

"Thank you."

"You're welcome."

The door opened wide and all the members of the Chamber of Commerce board plus the Mayor walked in the door. Val and Amy walked toward the group.

"Good Morning everyone, we have your tables all set up for you, if you will just follow me." Val headed for the center of the room.

"Amy and Chris will be your servers today and I have a fresh batch of cinnamon rolls for everyone."

"The decorations are cute," Rose said. "I love your Christmas tree. I can't wait 'til tonight to see your display, Val."

"I will tell you what I told my daughter Maggie, No peeking. I am going to get those rolls," Val winced when she started to walk.

Amy and Chris started to hand out the menus. Rose grabbed Amy's arm.

"Is Val's back still hurting her?" She asked.

"Yes."

"Good."

"Huh?"

"Not good that she is in pain but good for my plans."

"What plans?"

"You'll find out soon enough. Now I don't see any mistletoe in the place. Does she have any?"

"No, but I can sneak over to the florist and get some."

"Be a dear and do that for me."

"Okay, let me get the orders and out first," Amy said.

"By the way are you and Chris off tonight?"

"Yeah, Val is going to be here to hand out cookies and hot chocolate. Here she comes. So, what can I get for you today Ms. Rose?"

"I'll have the egg and cheese omelet with a side of bacon and coffee."

"Here you go everyone," Val put the platter of cinnamon rolls in the middle of the table.

James watched Val walking back toward the counter.

"Val, are you all right?" he asked.

"I will be when I can get some sleep."

"When will that be?"

"About the time Maggie gets married."

"Okay, just checking."

"More coffee?"

"Sure."

Mayor Robert leaned over the table and whispered to Rose, "Did I hear you ask for mistletoe? Are you trying to match up Val with someone?"

"Well, it worked for you and your wife."

"I know and may whoever you fix her up with be worthy of her and Maggie."

"Don't worry, I have a keen eye for these things. Now please pass the cinnamon rolls."

Amy and Chris walked over to the counter and handed Val the orders. Amy felt her phone buzzing in her pocket, she took it out and swiped the screen with her finger.

"Ben will be here in about half an hour and he wants to know if I have any sinus medicine." Amy smiled and texted back. "I will go to the drugstore when I get a minute and get you some." She grabbed the coffee pot and headed for the tables.

"Ms. Rose, Ben needs some sinus medicine so that is my excuse to get out of the building for a minute. Where should I hang it?"

"What time are you closing?"

"Six."

"I'll be back just before then."

Chapter Seven

As soon as all the chamber members were served, Val walked out of the kitchen with her own and Maggie's coat, plus Maggie's backpack.

"Come on little one, you've got a bus to catch."

"Oh, all right."

"I'll walk her to the bus stop," Amy said. "I have to run down to the drugstore and get some medicine for Ben and it is on the way. Rest your back for a minute."

"Oh, okay then."

Val buttoned Maggie's coat and watched as she put on her hat and gloves. She bent over and kissed her on the cheek. "Love you lots."

"Love you, Mama."

Val watched as she and Amy headed out the door. Rose walked over to the counter.

"She is so cute and smart as can be."

"She was asking me about her Dad last night."

"That must have been hard. But she is bound to be curious."

"Yeah... Oh, I almost forgot I have cookies for Carrie. Are you going to the hospital today?"

"Yes."

"I'll get go get them now before I forget." She disappeared behind the kitchen door.

Rose looked over at James. "You know," she started. "Val is going to be here tonight by herself during the festival, and I am sure she could use some extra help with everything. Especially since she is in so much pain. Plus, I bet there will be a huge crowd here, so you could get a story for the newspaper and help a damsel in distress."

The door opened, and Val emerged with cookie tins.

"I hope they like these," She handed the tins to Rose.

"I am sure they will." Rose looked at James again and he nodded and smiled.

Rose walked back to the Chamber of Commerce's table. She looked at the Mayor.

"Part one of the mission accomplished."

Fifteen minutes later Amy ran into the crowded florist shop. Even though she was out of breath she announced.

"I am a woman short on time and on a mistletoe mission."

Everyone in the store stopped what they were doing and stared at her.

"Oh, not for myself. It's for a friend. Not for a friend, but for someone who is trying to set up my friend for a little Christmas fling. I mean romance. Which we hope will turn into something better. Oh, nevermind I just need the mistletoe." She looked over at the clerk.

"What color ribbon would you like on that ma'am?"

"Red please."

Amy heard someone clear their throat, she turned and noticed her Priest standing over by the gift cards.

"Great, just great."

"That will be $10.95," The clerk said.

"For mistletoe?"

"It's the real stuff, not the stuff they have at the drugstore."

"Okay," Amy paid the clerk as she took the bag and headed for the door.

"Amy," her Priest called out.

"Yes Father, I will be in church on Sunday."

"Good answer."

A few minutes later Amy arrived at the diner. She peered through the door and Chris looked back at her. Not spying Val in the room, she quickly walked over to Rose.

"Mission accomplished."

"How much do I owe you dear?"

"If this works, nothing; if it doesn't $10.95."

"Deal."

Chris walked over to the table. "I know you are up to something."

"Amy was a dear and picked up something I needed from the florist. She saved this old woman from an extra errand. Thank you, dear."

"Humph." Chris snorted.

"We need to fix him up with someone next, Rose whispered.

"You need a miracle worker for that one."

"Now, Amy."

"Okay, I am already going to church because I ran into my Priest at the florist shop and I don't think he believes I am on a mission to fix up my friend for a long-term commitment."

"Amy, I am sure he has heard more interesting things during confession."

"In this town, I somehow doubt that."

"Just make sure you get Val out of here, so I can take care of things."

"How am I going to do that?"

"Remind her how Betsy dresses for this event."

"Can do."

Val walked into the dining room carrying cinnamon rolls for Amy and Chris.

"Hey, you two, I saved a couple of these for you and for Thomas when he gets here."

"What time will he be here?" Amy asked.

"He gets out of school at two. Probably by 2:15 or so."

"So how is the winner determined for tonight's festival?" James asked.

"The chamber board will be the judges and they vote for their favorites."

"Everyone walks to the Chamber of Commerce building and the winners are announced," Val answered.

"You know," Amy started. "Betsy always gets dressed up for this event every year. Last year she wore that red dress and carried a white fur muff. She looked like something out of the White Christmas movie."

"Are you hinting that I should go home and change out of my jeans and flannel shirt outfit?"

"Well maybe something a little more festive wouldn't hurt."

"Okay, I can take a hint. If things slow down this afternoon I will go home and change. Now after the chamber leaves, Chris can you set up the folding tables next to the jukebox, and Amy there are some red table clothes in my office along with paper plates and cups for the hot chocolate."

"Are you making Mexican hot chocolate this year?"

"No, I am making French hot chocolate for the adults and regular hot chocolate for the kids."

"Why two kinds?" James asked.

"French hot chocolate has espresso powder in it. I don't think parents would appreciate their kids having a caffeine high all night."

"Yeah, I don't think they would."

"Did you spend time in France during your travels?" James asked.

"Maggie and I were there for a few months. The apartment I rented was above a French bakery."

"Her opera cakes and her Poires Belle Helene are to die for," Amy said.

"What are Poires…. How do you say that again?"

"Poached pears with a sugar syrup, vanilla ice cream and chocolate sauce. That is how I put that on the menu. Most people around here could not pronounce it."

"I only make it for special occasions or holidays. I did make a batch last Halloween. The Chamber of Commerce hosts a Halloween dinner/party for grown-ups."

"Are you going to make it for the employee Christmas party this year?"

"I may or I might make Mantecados instead."

"What's that?" Chris asked.

"Spanish crumb cake," James answered.

"How did you know that?"

"My Mom's neighbors are from Spain and she makes them every Christmas."

"Did you have a traditional Christmas dinner growing up?"

"My Mom is Italian, and my Father was Cherokee. So, for Thanksgiving we would have a traditional turkey dinner, but for Christmas my Mom is all about the homemade Panettone cake and we have dinner on Christmas Eve. Usually seafood and salads type things."

"Isn't that called the feast of the seven fishes?" Val asked.

"Yeah, that's right."

"What is a Panettone cake?" Amy asked.

"A cake with fruit in it."

"Like a fruitcake?" Chris turned up his nose.

"Much better than the American version of a fruitcake. It is very good."

"Have you made it before?" James asked.

"It was my husband's favorite cake. I used to make it for his birthday." Val looked at the floor.

"I'm sorry, I didn't mean to upset you."

"You couldn't have known."

"I better see if the chamber table needs more coffee," Amy grabbed the coffee pot and headed for the table. She looked at Rose and leaned over.

"You may need more mistletoe," she whispered.

"Why?"

"James sort of inserted his foot into his mouth. Unintentionally reminding Val of her husband."

"This time of year, is hard on her anyway with all of the old memories."

"Are you sure we should try to fix her up with James?"

"She needs love back in her life. Desperately, and some laughter."

"Okay then."

"I will get more mistletoe on the way home from the hospital. Plus, I am going to bring by some dinner and candles. Does she have any candle holders around here?"

"I don't think so."

Chris came up behind them "You two are up to something; now what is it?"

"Just talking about going to church on Sunday."

"Humph." Chris walked away.

"With all of this, I may need to go to confession on Wednesday."

"Amy, there is nothing wrong with arranging a little romantic surprise."

"Tell that to our priest."

Amy walked toward the counter areas.

"Are they going to leave soon?" Val asked.

"I think they were starting to wrap up."

"Good, I have to get lunch started." Val attempted to stretch. "Ouch, Ouch, Ouch."

"You need to relax boss," Chris said.

"No, I need to take care of things, so no rest for the utterly exhausted."

James stood up and grabbed his wallet from his back pocket.

"I'll get your check," Amy volunteered. "That will be $6.50."

James pulled the money out of his pocket and put the tip down on the counter. "I will see you all tonight." He looked directly at Val.

"Have a great day," Val answered. James walked out the door.

Val started toward the kitchen door. "Oh, before I forget, whoever is considering buying a puppy for my daughter for Christmas, that person will have to train that puppy. Understand?" She went into the kitchen.

Rose walked up to the counter. "Amy, how much do we owe you?"

"That will be $74.15 for everybody."

Rose handed her the money. "Don't worry, I will make sure Chris is gone early too."

"How?" Amy whispered.

"Hal is going to need some extra help this evening."

Rose walked into the inn carrying bags from the grocery store and from the florist. Hal was stoking up the fire in the living room and he turned and looked over at her.

"Do you have more bags in the car?"

"Yes, I have grocery bags in the trunk."

Hal put the fireplace poker back on the stand and walked toward the entrance. Once he got there, he looked down at one of the bags and noticed some mistletoe peeking out of it.

"I see you got some mistletoe. Is that for here or someplace else?"

"Both, and I also picked up some holly sprigs from the florist to decorate the chandelier in the dining room. Which reminds me, you are going to need some help with that."

"When am I putting this up?"

"Tonight."

"I thought we were going to the festival tonight."

"We are and at 5:30 today, I am going to call Chris and ask for his help with this."

"You are?"

"Yes, now I have to get busy in the kitchen, so please bring in the rest of the bags."

"You are up to something."

"Of course, it's the holidays."

"Is any of this mistletoe staying here?"

"Of course. But I don't think Chris will want to help you with that."

With a big smile, Hal winked at Rose, then said, "I understand the reasons why dear."

"Don't forget your coat."

"I won't."

He grabbed his coat and headed out the door. Once he got to the car, he popped open the trunk and noticed one of the bags had spilled over and a bottle of red wine had rolled out. He picked it up and looked at the label.

"That is not the brand she uses to make mulled wine," He mumbled and dug a little more into the bags. "Italian bread, diced tomatoes, spaghetti, garlic, onion, herbs, ground beef. She is making her homemade spaghetti and meatballs."

Hal walked into the kitchen with the bags as Rose was getting the standing mixer out of the cabinet.

"I hope you are going to save some of that spaghetti for us. Nobody makes homemade sauce like you do." He came up behind her and gave her a little hug.

"Of course, I can't forget my best guy."

"I saw the wine also, isn't that one of Val's favorite brands?"

"Yes."

"I hope those two have a romantic evening and maybe we can have one after the festival." He hugged her again.

"Stop that! I have work to do."

Val walked into her living room a little before 5:00 p.m. Amy had insisted that she go home and get fixed up for the festival. Luckily Amy volunteered to watch Maggie and fix her dinner while Val took this little break. She put her coat on the hook and headed for her bedroom. What do I wear that is festive enough? And doesn't look tacky?

First, she pulled out the ugly Christmas sweater she wore to the employee Christmas party last year. "No way," she mumbled. Somehow the abominable light up snowman didn't seem appropriate. Her white cashmere sweater was too fancy, and she didn't want to worry about chocolate being spilled on it. The red blouse, too thin for winter. She pulled out a burgundy sweater that her mother gave her last Christmas and laid it on her bed.

"Perfect, now what jewelry."

In her jewelry box she rummaged through it until she found her Grandmother's antique Christmas tree pin. She put it next to her sweater. She opened her closet door again and searched for black dress pants.

"Shoot, I forgot to wash my black dress pants." She chose a long black skirt with a matching black and gold belt, plus her black dress shoes. "This will have to do." Upon checking her watch, she mentally figured she had enough time for a soaking bath. She draped the clothes on the bed and headed for the bathroom.

"One bath coming up." She opened the cabinet to get a towel and saw an unopened bottle of Shalimar perfume. *Why not pamper myself.* Putting the bottle on the counter next to her make-up bag, she started to close the cabinet door and noticed a candle on one of the shelves. Where did I put the matches?

At 5:30 p.m. Rose was in the dining room getting candleholders off the table when she saw James out of the corner of her eye coming down the stairs carrying his coat.

"Hello James, where are you heading to this evening?"

"I thought I would head to the pub for a bit to eat before the festival tonight."

"Oh, um they closed up early today. The owner is a member of the Chamber of Commerce, so he will be meeting up early to get things ready for tonight. In fact, I will be leaving here in a few minutes."

"Where is a good place to get something to eat then?"

"I am sure Val will have some food at the diner when the festival starts at 7 tonight. Plus, with her back still hurting I am sure she can use some extra help with everything."

"She needs to hire more help."

"Well, some of her waitresses are out of town right now. I think they come back later this week. Hal would help her out, but he is going to be with me."

"Okay, I'll stop by the diner and see what I can do to help her out."

"There are some sugar cookies and hot coffee in the living room, that should tide you over till then."

James walked into the living room after he gathered some cookies and sat down in one of the chairs, Rose gathered up the candleholders and headed for the kitchen. She picked up the phone and punched in the diner's phone number.

"Hello Chris, this is Rose. Hal needs your help with something."

"What's that?"

"Well we are having some special guests arriving tomorrow and I need to have the dining room fixed up for their wedding anniversary dinner. Could you be a dear and help Hal with fixing up the chandelier? The ladder he has is so old and I am afraid that he will fall and wind up in the emergency room. Remember last year when he wound up in the emergency room?"

"I can come by tomorrow before work."

"We need to get this done tonight. Tomorrow is Hal's day to volunteer at the nursing home. I will be at the church getting their decorations ready for the handbell choir festival."

"It is kind of quiet here. Let me see if Amy can close up and then I will be right over."

"Thank you, dear." She hung up the phone.

"I am telling so many fibs, if I keep this up, I may have to stop by confession tomorrow," she whispered.

Chapter Eight

At 6:00 p.m. Rose parked her car in front of the diner, walked over to the door and peered inside. Amy saw her and waved back for her to come in. Rose waved for her to come to the door instead and Rose walked back to her car and popped the trunk. She picked up one crate of food as Amy made it to the car.

"Did you bring enough food for the entire diner?" Amy asked.

"No, I brought things to set a romantic mood."

"A romantic mood when the whole town will be stopping by for cookies, hot chocolate and to judge the window."

"The tour starts at the other end of the street and it will take a while for people to get here, so help me get all of this inside."

"Okay," Amy grabbed the bags of mistletoe and the other bag of items and headed for the door.

Rose held the door open for Amy, and then headed for the kitchen barking orders as she went.

"Amy please put those bags down anywhere and please go close my trunk. I am going to put the dinner on the stove, and can you move two tables together."

Then she noticed Maggie sitting at the counter eating a hamburger. "Hi Maggie," She headed on into the kitchen and put the crate on the counter.

"Can I help you, ma'am?" Thomas came up behind her.

"Thomas!" Rose put her hand on her heart. "Don't ever sneak up on an old lady like that."

"Why are you in the kitchen?"

"I am preparing a little surprise for Ms. Val. Sort of a Christmas miracle. Now if you can get a big pot for me to put the spaghetti noodles in, that would be great, and I need another one to heat up the sauce."

"Okay,"

"I promise I will clean this up before I leave."

"Do you want me to put the noodles in now?"

"No, I will get that going in a minute."

Rose walked into the dining area and immediately noticed that Amy had set the romantic table complete with the red tablecloth, candles and wine glasses. She walked over to Maggie.

"Maggie, aren't you going to the festival tonight?"

"Yes, ma'am. I am going with Amy and Ben. What are you doing?"

"Well, since your Mom is so nice to everyone and she works so hard all the time. Amy and I thought we would cook her dinner tonight as sort of a surprise."

"So, are you one of Santa's special elves too? Like me?"

"What do special Santa elves do?" Amy asked.

"They keep a giving advent calendar, each day they have to do something nice for someone. Like give gift cards to complete strangers or bake cookies for someone."

"Yeah, I guess you could say that." Rose cautiously looked at Amy.

"Yes, you could say that. Can you keep this a secret and no calling or texting your mom?"

"My mom won't let me have a cellphone."

"Okay than," Amy said. "Rose where do you want me to hang the mistle... I mean the decorations?"

"When is Val due back?"

"At quarter of seven."

"Okay, so I have to get back to the kitchen."

"Hang one branch over the table on the light fixture, a twig over the main door, a twig over the cash register and the last branch on the light fixture over by the jukebox."

"You've got a lot of decorations."

"I am not leaving anything to chance." Rose walked back into the kitchen.

"Okay," Amy said. "Maggie you need to finish your burger and fries."

"Yes, ma'am. Can I have a cookie?"

"After dinner."

"Okay," she moaned.

Rose noticed that Thomas had filled the large pot with water for her when he asked.

"Can I help you with something else?"

"You can chop the vegetables up for the salad and put the rolls on plates for me. Is that okay?"

"Yes ma'am, I cook at home for my brothers and sisters."

"Will they be at the festival tonight?"

"No, ma'am, Mom has to work. I must make sure my brothers and sisters have done their homework, get their baths, and ready for bed. Plus do my homework."

"That is a lot for a young man to take care of."

"I just do it to help Mom out."

"Okay, well I better get this spaghetti going here."

Rose watched for a moment as Thomas started chopping up the vegetables.

"This young man and his family need one of Santa's special elves." She whispered to herself.

Val pulled into a parking space behind the diner at 6:45 p.m. When she got out of her van, she almost slipped on the frozen ground.

"Dang dress shoes." She cautiously crept to the back door and unlocked it. Once she walked inside the scent of tomato sauce filled her nose. *That's weird.* She flipped on the light and headed for her office, hurriedly put her purse on her desk and hung up her coat. *Whoever invented high heels should be tortured. My feet and back hurt already.* She bent down, adjusted the strap around her ankle and headed out the door toward the dining area. *Something is not right.* She ran her hand along the wall to find the switch and turned on the lights. Her eyes immediately noticed several bunches of mistletoe hanging in different places around the room. *Okay, what else is going on here?* She headed for the front door and paused when she saw the table made up for dinner. Two place settings, candlelight and wine. An envelope on the table. Val opened it up and pulled out the note.

"We thought you two deserved a nice dinner."

"I have an idea who 'the we' are but what other person are they talking about."

Just then she heard a tapping noise on the front door, turned around and saw James. She immediately felt the flush rise to her cheeks. Taking a deep breath, she walked towards the door and turned the latch.

"Hi," Val tilted her head down hoping James would not notice her flaming cheeks.

"Hi, Rose said you may need some help this evening with all of the festivities."

"Come on in," Val stepped aside as he walked in. "Here, I will hang up your coat." James took off his coat and handed it to her. "I am afraid that Rose may have had a different idea for this evening," Val said as she hung up his coat.

"What do you mean?"

"The table and the mistletoe."

James glanced around the room and spotted all the mistletoe bunches and then he noticed the table.

"It seems like we have been set up for some sort of dinner date," Val added.

"Now I understand why Rose told me the pub was closed. How long before the crowd makes its way here?"

"Probably about forty minutes to an hour."

James pointed to the tables by the jukebox. "Would you like to have it be a quick dinner? It looks like you have everything set up."

"Yeah, I know this was unexpected. You don't have to stay if you don't want to."

James walked over to the table and lifted the silver cover from the plate.

"It would be a shame to let all of this good food go to waste." He put the cover back down and picked up the wine bottle. "Hey, someone has good taste in wine. Shall we?"

He pulled a chair out for Val and she walked over to the table.

"Thank you." She sat down, still a little nervous about the evening.

"By the way, you look amazing."

"Thank you."

"How about some music?"

"All right."

James went to the jukebox and scrolled through the songs. He punched in several buttons then walked back towards Val. *Nevertheless, I'm in Love with You* started playing.

"Are you a Dean Martin fan?" Val asked.

"I am a fan of some of the classics and you?"

"I am a fan of the classics also. Well, I am a rocker also."

"Evident by the Gun and Roses, Nirvana and Santana CDs in the jukebox. Would you like some wine?"

"Yes, please." She watched James start to pour the wine in her glass.

"I could get used to being served dinner in my own restaurant."

James lifted his glass, "Here is to a fun evening and may you win the blue ribbon."

Val lifted her glass and clinked it to his.

"This spaghetti sauce smells wonderful."

"Probably Rose's homemade sauce."

"Is it one of your recipes?"

"No, that one is hers. But the rolls are probably my recipe."

"My mother makes her own sauce also." James took a bite of the spaghetti.

"So how does this compare?"

"Close but not as good as Mom's."

"You are loyal."

James twirled his spaghetti for a moment as Val took a sip of wine.

"How did you wind up in Festive?"

Val put down her wine glass and stared at her plate for a moment.

"After my husband died, things got rough for me in New York."

"Rough? How?"

"His parents blamed me for the accident. One of our neighbors told reporters that we had an argument that morning. I was so mad. She neglected to say that the day before she saw us laughing, putting up Christmas decorations on our porch and playing with Maggie in the snow. But anyway, my in-laws filed for custody of Maggie. Reporters followed us around for days before, during, and after the hearing. I am not a big fan of reporters; Funny thing was what we argued about that morning."

"What was that?"

"My, husband wanted to move to Connecticut and start his own business. He hated working for his father. He felt like I was spending too much time working and not enough time with Maggie. I wanted to wait another year because I would have been on better footing for opening my own restaurant or getting an executive chef position at another restaurant.

"Better footing?"

"I was the sous chef at the Purple Bayou Restaurant. I wanted to be a chef at a fancy restaurant. I enjoyed what I was doing."

"Where did you meet your husband?"

"The culinary school that I attended catered several charity events. I was monitoring the dessert table a charity ball. Rich asked me who made the nonnettes. I told him I did, and we started talking."

"Nonnettes?"

"French ginger cake."

"Then how did you wind up here?"

"I wasn't planning on it. I knew Maggie needed stability and I decided to move back to the states. I did not want to spend Christmas in New York, so we stayed at the Holly Inn. Rose and Hal became great friends. I stayed on through January and this place came on the market. I bought a small log cabin house and it took about three months for renovations to be completed and here we are. Now you know my story. What is yours?"

"I got married seven years ago. My ex-wife had an affair and we got divorced four years ago."

"Ouch, that had to hurt."

"Honestly, I think I wanted the marriage more than she did. We were too different. Shortly after my divorce my father passed away and my mother had several physical issues. I moved in with her to keep an eye on things."

"Do you have any children?"

"No."

Val sensed the subject should be changed from the sad look on James' face.

"Well right before the crowd gets here, the Christmas Crier arrives. We have about five minutes to get everything in place. Once they get here, we pull back the curtains and invite everyone in."

"With all of this mistletoe around here, you may have a few romances going on before the night is over."

"Oh boy, well how about I clear these dishes away first."

"Here let me get that." He got up and headed for the counter area.

"Wow, you are spoiling me."

"That's the plan."

Val got up and walked over to the cookie table. She ran her fingers across the tablecloth.

"Would you like some cookies?"

"Not now."

James put the dishes into the grey plastic tub, while Val walked over to the jukebox and started going through the music list. She punched in some numbers. *Baby, It's Cold Outside* started to play. James came up beside her.

"May I have this dance?"

"Okay. It has been a long time since I danced in high heels."

"Just like riding a bike." James took her hand and put his other hand around her waist.

Val tripped, and she laughed.

"Maybe not that easy."

"Just relax."

"Are you going to the movie festival? There will be lots of food and games for the kids in the lobby."

"That depends."

"On what?"

"Will you be my date?"

"I will have my daughter with me."

"That will work."

"Okay then."

"I will pick you two up at six." Just then James twirled Val around and leaned her into a dip.

"Oh, whoops" She laughed, and he lifted her back up. Very close to each other, everything got quiet and he leaned in for a kiss.

"Hear ye, hear ye, the festival has arrived at the Memories Diner," The Crier announced.

"I better go get everything ready."

"Yeah."

Amy, Ben, Maggie, Rose and Hal walked along the festival route. Amy had a Styrofoam cup of hot chocolate in her hand. Maggie had on a purple coat and white earmuffs and a strange expression on her face. Chris was a few paces away from the group.

"Maggie is something wrong? Are you cold?" Rose asked.

"No, ma'am. What does garish mean?" she asked.

"I believe it means tasteless or gaudy. Why do you ask?"

"Mr. Baxter said that about Ms. Betsy's window."

Amy tried not to laugh, and she started to choke on her hot chocolate.

"Let's not be too loud about that dear," Rose said.

"He was right. It looked more like a Vegas stage show with that Elvis mannequin dressed in that white costume. That silver garland curtain and all the blue lights and ornaments," Hal said.

"What window do you like so far, Ben?" Rose tried to change the subject.

"The window at the Harvest bank is pretty cool. I liked the theme."

"Elves day off," Amy said. "I must admit the elf dolls on top of the snow hill skiing and the polar bears building a snow fort is pretty cute. Plus, the apple caramel snacks were pretty good. But the hot chocolate is a store-bought mix."

"We're almost at the diner, so we can get some real hot chocolate there," Hal said.

Amy nervously looked at Rose.

"I wonder how our new decorations went over," Amy said.

"I bet everything went fine."

"It better have, or I am going to be on dish duty for a week."

"What did you do?" Ben asked.

"Never you mind, Ben." Rose interrupted.

"They are playing matchmaker." Hal inserted.

"What is a matchmaker?" Maggie asked.

"Now look what you started." Rose jokingly scolded Hal.

They arrived at the diner as Val was opening the door. James walked out the door holding his camera. He looked at Maggie and smiled.

"Good Evening Everyone," Val called out. "Welcome to the Memories Diner."

"Good Evening Ms. Val, would you please tell us the theme of your window this year?" The Christmas Crier asked.

"It is Santa's Workshop."

"Please pull back the curtain."

"Of course." She walked back into the diner and pulled the curtain rope. The curtains slowly opened. She could hear the crowd's praiseful ahs and oohs, through the window. She walked outside.

"Look, the screen lights up," Ben said.

"Please come in everyone, for some cookies and hot chocolate," Val invited.

Rose and Amy approached the door. Val leaned in to greet them.

"You two have some explaining to do. Tell me did you have anything to do with the little surprise that is inside?"

"What surprise?"

"That is what I thought."

About to close the door, Val looked over and saw Mr. Jeffers standing on his front porch. That's a first. She waved at him to come over and he shook his head no. She closed the door and walked back inside. She was heading toward the jukebox to punch in more Christmas tunes when she noticed that the table had been reset and the candle was lit. James stood next to her.

"What's with all of the mistletoe?" the Mayor asked.

"Val decided to have two themes this year," James announced, noticing a blush rising in Val's face. "The Santa workshop and Christmas romance. Just a little idea for us guys to take care of the women in our lives who do so much for our families during the holidays."

"Thank You," Val whispered in his ear.

"I get it," Ben announced. "Take them out to dinner and get some wine."

"Or you could cook dinner for them," Hal added.

"Since the only thing you can cook is scrambled eggs, I think you will be taking me out to dinner," Rose added.

"See what you have started Val. Now all of us will have to do something for our wives." Mayor Rob added.

"Yes, and your idea should include her favorite chocolates," Rose laughed.

"All right, I get it." The Mayor laughed.

"Please everyone help yourselves to some cookies and hot chocolate," Val said. She walked over to the jukebox and punched in the numbers for *Baby It's Cold Outside, Winter Wonderland* and *I Saw Mommy Kissing Santa Claus.*

"Mommy can I have some cookies?"

"You can have three cookies and some hot chocolate."

Val walked over to the table and handed Maggie a plate. She got a cup and started to ladle out the hot chocolate for her.

"Friday Mr. James is coming to the movies with us, and I think I found a way to pull off one of our Christmas surprises," she whispered to her daughter.

"Which one?" Maggie whispered back.

"One idea for Mr. Jeffers," Val whispered in her ear.

"Okay."

"Here is your hot chocolate so please go sit down at one of the tables."

"Yes, ma'am."

Rose and Amy walked over to Val as she was serving hot chocolate to the other guests.

"Are you mad at us?" Amy asked tentatively.

"No, I am not mad at you and thankfully James saved the night so to speak. However, I do expect that all but one of these bunches of mistletoe will be down when I come into work tomorrow."

"Which one gets to stay up?" Rose asked.

"The bunch by the jukebox."

"Okay, boss."

"Where is Chris?"

"Betsy cornered him over by the cash register. I bet she is trying to get his secret on that lighted canvas."

"Amy, why don't you go get Chris and save him from that woman?"

Mr. and Mrs. Baxter walked over to the table and gathered a few cookies.

"I always look forward to your desserts," Mrs. Baxter said as she took a bite out of one of them. "Divine."

"Thank you, Now tell me about Betsy's window?"

"Utterly garish," Mr. Baxter added. "All silver and blue with a giant Elvis. Your real competition this year was the window at the bank."

"What was their theme?"

"Elves day off."

"That is a cute idea."

James walked back over to the cookie table and he placed his hand on the small part of Val's back. Startled by the intimate gesture, she jumped but smiled at him. A glance at Rose and Val knew the woman caught the gentle touch.

"I have been working the crowd and your window is a hit." He whispered to Val.

"You think so?"

"Yeah,"

"I may have a special mission for us to complete on Friday night after we go to the movies."

"Okay."

"I have to double-check the movie schedule first."

"Now I am intrigued."

"Santa's elves are always at work."

"It is almost time to move to the Hardware store." The Christmas Crier announced.

"Shall we?" James asked.

"As soon as I can lock up, we shall."

"I need to get my gloves out of my car, so I'll wait for you outside."

"All right then."

C✍Chapter Nine✍⊃

Val grabbed her keys from her office desk and walked into the main dining area. She looked around the room giving it one more check to see if she unplugged the now empty crockpots. She put her coat on and walked out the door and she saw James leaning against his car.

"I just need to lock up." She turned and locked the door, as James walked over towards her.

"The crowd is at the florists. If we hurry, we can catch up to them."

Val started walking slowly. "Nah, let's take our time." She took a deep breath. "I love this time of night."

"Why is that?"

"It is quiet, and when you have a child, quiet time is precious. This town at night is usually so peaceful and that is a far cry from New York."

"Or Chicago."

"Would you ever leave Chicago?"

"I thought about it when I first got divorced. But after Dad died, well I could not leave Mom there alone. She sent me a text earlier. She is having dinner tonight with a neighbor gentleman Harvey, and then they are going to watch a movie."

"Is Mr. Harvey a widower?"

"Yes."

"Your Mom is on a date."

"What? Nah."

"Will wine be served?"

"Probably."

"Wine, dinner and a movie equal a date."

"No."

"Do not tell me that you are one of those guys that freaks about his Mother having a life."

"I didn't think I was."

Val laughed and then her foot hit a patch of ice and she started sliding. James grabbed her arm and steadied her.

"Dang these shoes."

"Not exactly snow proof."

"I forgot my boots."

"Here then," James held out his arm. "Lean on me."

Val tentatively put her arm in his and leaned against his shoulder.

"Would you ever move back to New York?"

"I don't think so"

"Bad memories?"

"That and here we are anonymous, no reporters taking pictures as I walk down the street. One of them was so bad he came right up to Maggie's stroller and started snapping pictures of her. He scared her so much she started screaming.

Nothing against New York but here it is peaceful, and it is a good place to raise Maggie. Plus, I don't miss the rat-race anymore, the noise and don't get me started on the traffic."

"I guess there are not many traffic jams in Festive."

"No, just on the interstate sometimes."

A few minutes later the crowd emptied out of the florist shop and started walking toward the Chamber of Commerce building. Amy and the rest of the group were among the last to walk out the door. She turned toward Rose.

"Have you seen Val or James?" Amy asked.

Rose looked over her shoulder. "They are walking this way. Don't turn, they are walking arm in arm. Looks like romance is in the air," Rose whispered.

"Ladies," Hal started "We better get over to the Chamber for the vote tally."

Maggie peered out from the middle of the group and noticed her Mom and James walking toward them.

"Mommy, we went to the flower shop and I ate a whole chocolate rose."

"Great, more sugar on a school night."

"Can we watch a movie when we get home?"

"No, when we get home, you are going to have a warm bath and then go to sleep."

Maggie started to pout.

"Come on, little one let's head over to the Chamber building." Val looked at James. "The joys of parenthood."

She saw a crowd starting to gather around the Chamber Christmas tree. The Mayor and his wife approached the podium. James pulled up his camera and started taking pictures.

"Did you take a picture of my display?"

"Of course, I did."

"You will have to email it to me, so I can have a copy."

"Deal."

"Good evening everyone." The Mayor started. "I want to thank everyone for turning out this evening. It has been a wonderful stroll through our downtown area. I want to thank every one of the business owners for such fine decorations and Christmas treats this evening. I ate way too many Christmas cookies. I am just waiting for Rose to bring over the results of tonight's contest. The winner, of course, gets the blue ribbon, a basket filled with Christmas goodies, and bragging rights for the next year." Rose walked over to the podium and gave the Mayor a white index card. "Okay, in third place and winner of the white ribbon is G C's Candy store for their reindeer flying school display." George Collins walked over to the podium and shook the Mayor's hand and Rose handed him the ribbon. "Okay in second place and winner of the Red ribbon is Harvest Bank for their Elves Day Off display. Jay, come on up here and get your ribbon." Jay shook the Mayor's hand and Rose handed him the ribbon.

Val glanced up at James and then at Maggie. She felt the heat of someone staring at her and skimmed a glance over the crowd and she noticed Betsy glaring at her. *If looks could kill, I would have a thousand arrows in me right now.*

"Okay folks the first-place winner is Memories Diner for their Santa's workshop display. Well done, Val."

"Yay Mommy," Maggie yelled.

"Come up here Val and get your ribbon."

Val walked up to the podium, and the Mayor gave her the basket and ribbon. "Thank you, Mr. Mayor, and thank you to all of the Chamber members." She walked back down towards James and Maggie.

"Well everyone, on behalf of the Chamber, congratulations to all of the winners. Thank you again for coming out and be careful driving home. Goodnight."

As the group started quietly walking back toward the diner, James walked close to Val in case she started to slip again. Maggie was carrying the blue ribbon. Chris was a few steps behind the crowd watching James.

"Mommy, are you going to hang your ribbon on the wall?"

"No, I think I will just put it back in my office."

"But you won."

"Yes, but a lady doesn't gloat."

"What does gloat mean?"

"It means brag." James smiled and almost laughed.

"Oh."

Rose tapped Val on her shoulder to get her attention, "Did you see Wallace Singleton?"

"No."

"He was there taking pictures."

"Who is Wallace Singleton?"

"A reporter for the local newspaper."

"I guess that means he will be at the diner tomorrow." Val sighed.

"Okay so if he comes in, it's only for pictures of the window, no pictures of me or Maggie and he can only use my first name in any articles. Okay everyone?"

"Okay," Amy answered.

"Mommy are we going home soon?" Maggie asked.

"We have to straighten up the diner then we will go home."

"Mommy?"

'Yes?"

"My tummy hurts."

"Okay, that happens when you eat too many sweets. Let's get back to the diner and get you some water."

Once they reached the diner Val unlocked the door and turned on the lights. Everyone walked inside.

James was hanging up his coat when Val stopped him.

"James, you don't have to stay."

"I would like to help out so put me to work."

Chris scoffed behind him.

Val put the basket and ribbon down on one of the tables

"Okay, everyone" She paused while the group turned and looked at her.

"I have to take care of Maggie, she's not feeling very well, so Chris could you gather up the dishes and take them to the back James could you and Hal you put the folding tables in the storage room Amy and Rose, can you take care of removing the extra decorations And Ben could take the trash out please Amy please put this basket and ribbon in my office."

"Mommy my stomach really hurts."

"Okay honey; let's go back to the bathroom first."

They quickly headed out of the room. James watched them for a moment. Hal walked up behind him, but James was still staring at the door.

"Hey, earth to James." Hal snapped his fingers.

"Yeah," James answered.

"You got it bad."

"Where do the tables go?"

"Come on."

The group got started on their chores. Amy and Rose were busy removing the extra decorations.

"I wonder if this worked," Amy said.

"From the way those two are acting, I dare say something started this evening."

"Yeah, but I feel bad Maggie is sick."

"She will be fine. Kids and adults overindulge a little this season."

"Are you going to the Hand Bell concert?"

"No."

"Hal and I have some serious Christmas shopping to do tomorrow and then we are getting everything ready for the Give Back Festival."

A few minutes later Val and Maggie emerged from the back room. Maggie was carrying a water bottle and looking a little pale.

"Go sit at the counter for a moment and drink your water."

"Yes, ma'am."

Val surveyed the room and noticed Amy and Rose taking down the last bit of the mistletoe but leaving one bunch by the jukebox like she asked. The rest of the chores had been finished by the group.

"Amy, can you open up tomorrow. I will be coming in a little later. I just want to make sure Maggie gets a little extra sleep."

"Sure."

"I can come in early if you need me to," Chris volunteered.

"I think Amy can handle it. Thanks anyway. I better get her home. So, Chris can you lock up?"

"Sure."

"Thank you everyone for helping out tonight. Goodnight everyone."

"Goodnight," said the group in unison.

Val walked over toward Maggie and touched her shoulder.

"Come on, sweetie, time to head home."

They walked out the backdoor. Val opened the van sliding door, and Maggie got into the backseat.

"Buckle up."

"Val," James said.

Val jumped "Oh, you scared me."

"I am sorry."

"Is there something you need?"

"I just wanted to say goodnight and I hope Maggie feels better."

"Thank you, goodnight."

James opened the car door for Val after she climbed in, he shut the door.

"Be careful going home."

"I will, and be careful driving back to the inn."

"Goodnight."

"Goodnight, James."

Val started up the van and James took a step back as she started backing up. She saw him watching for a moment as she drove out of the parking lot.

A lavender bath and two stories later Val was sitting on the edge of Maggie's bed. She reached over and brushed some of the hair from Maggie's forehead.

"Are you feeling better?"

"Yes, ma'am."

"You get to sleep in a little longer tomorrow morning. But you will still have breakfast at the diner."

"Okay."

"Goodnight and sweet dreams."

"Sweet dreams to you too, Mama."

Val got up and walked over to the door.

"Mama?"

"Yes?"

"I'm glad you won."

"Goodnight sweetie." She turned out the light and was about halfway down the hall when she felt her phone vibrate in her pocket. She pulled it out and noticed she had a text message. *Now what.* She opened the message saw it was from James.

"Hey, I got your number from Rose. I hope you don't mind. How is Maggie feeling?"

"Better, Thank you." Val turned off her phone and sat down on the couch.

She pulled her laptop off the coffee table. *Time to do some Christmas ordering.*

Chapter Ten

James was back in his hotel room when he opened his phone and read Val's message. He put the phone down next to his computer and opened his laptop. He pulled up his email account. The first message he read was from his mother. She described what a wonderful evening she had at Harvey's and that she was going Christmas shopping with one of their other neighbors. The second email he opened was from his boss, Bryon.

"Just reminding you that you have a Friday midnight deadline for this Sunday's issue. What is going on with the Val Young story? You need something more than just a pretty lights story."

James punched in "I will make the deadline. I don't know about the Val Young story. She does not like or trust reporters. Especially after the way she was treated by them in New York. She hates the fact that they would come out of nowhere and scare her daughter."

James was downloading pictures from his camera onto his computer when another mail message popped up on his screen. He opened the message from Bryon.

"Do you want to remain on the style page forever? If so, tell me now. Val Young is the real story here. She was the upcoming chef that won awards and people were anticipating that she would have her own show on one of those cooking channels. Married to the heir of a fortune that tragically died. And then she disappeared. Now get me this story or expect to be covering fashion shows for a very long time."

James pulled up the pictures he had just downloaded and looked at the ones he had taken of Val. He opened a new file. Val Young private he typed in for a file name and then moved all the pictures of her to that folder. He turned off his laptop without responding to his boss's email.

"I don't want to stay on the style page," he muttered.

At 7:00 a.m. the next morning Val grabbed her second cup of coffee from the counter and headed for her daughter's room. She quietly opened the door. She walked in and put the cup down on Maggie's dresser. She moved over to her daughter's bed and tapped her on the shoulder.

"Wake up sleepy head." She smiled when Maggie stirred and tried to ignore her mother's voice.

"Come on get up. You have to go to school."

"But I don't want to." Maggie moaned.

"Hey kiddo, guess what, that's life, so get up now and head for the bathroom. I let you sleep in so move it." Val got up and pulled down the covers.

"It's not fair," Maggie said as she slowly got out of bed and headed for her door. "Grownups get to do whatever they want."

Val picked up her cup of coffee then followed Maggie out of the room. "Yeah right," she whispered. *You have a lot to learn Maggie dear.*

Half an hour later Maggie walked into the living room carrying her backpack. Val stood at the sink in the kitchen area washing her coffee mug. "Did you pack your books?"

"Yes, ma'am."

"Do you have pencils?"

"Yes, ma'am."

Val picked up a paper sack from the counter. "I packed your lunch today. No trading for candy today or else you'll get sick again and miss play practice." She handed Maggie the bag.

"I don't want to miss practice. No trading I promise." Maggie crossed her heart.

"Go open the box on the advent calendar."

Maggie went over to the kitchen table, crawled up into her chair, reached over, pulled open the door, and got the piece of paper from inside.

"What does it say?"

"Be Santa's secret helper and give a Christmas ornament to someone to brighten their day."

"Santa's secret helper, who should we give an ornament to?"

"Mrs. Betsy."

"Why Mrs. Betsy?"

"She looked sad last night when she lost."

"Out of the mouths of babes," Val whispered.

"Huh?"

"Go get an ornament out of the gift basket and I will get the gift box and tags."

Val pulled a small gift box with a tag out of the cupboard by the front door.

Maggie went over to the gift basket on the fireplace hearth and picked out a white and pink teapot ornament. She handed it to Val.

"Okay, go get your coat, hat and gloves please."

Val wrapped the ornament in tissue, put it in the box, and attached the tag which she had previously written.

Merry Christmas from Santa's secret elves.

"Maggie, come on, let's go." She yelled.

Ten minutes later Val parked the van in the alley behind Betsy's shop. She got out of the van and looked around before opening the door.

"Okay, Secret elf, do you have the gift?"

"Yes, Secret elf Mama."

Val smiled. "Okay, go put it by that blue door." Val pointed to the door "Remember no one can see or hear us."

Maggie carefully walked over to the door and put the gift down in that space where the sidewalk met the door. Then she walked back to the van.

"Come on, we better get a move on before someone sees us," Val said.

They got in the van and Maggie buckled her seatbelt. Val put the van in drive and headed towards Main Street.

"That was fun, Mom."

"I hope someday when you have children, you will teach them how to be secret elves too." Val smiled.

"Did Grandma teach you?"

"Yes."

"Did her Mom teach her?"

"You will have to ask her that question when she comes to visit."

"I wish she was coming for Christmas."

"Me too honey. But she has to spend some time with her brother. Remember your Uncle Peter? Well, he has been sick, and he needs a little help right now. But she will be here for New Years, so you will get two Christmases this year."

"Is Santa coming two times?"

"No, you will have your regular Christmas with me, and Santa comes to that one, and then you will have one with your Grandma."

"Okay, that works."

"You are a funny one, Maggie Sue."

Val parked the van in her spot behind the diner. "Come on, time to get your breakfast and off to school you will go."

They walked hand in hand into the diner. Val quickly surveyed the room and saw that everything was set up for the day. Amy was putting out the last of the salt and pepper shakers.

"Good morning, Amy," Maggie said.

"Good morning Maggie, how are you feeling?

"Better."

"Good morning Amy. Everything looks great. While I write the specials on the board can you unlock the front door?"

"What are the specials today?" Amy asked and headed for the door.

"Sausage gravy with biscuits, French toast with berries and white chocolate, Corned beef hash with two eggs and toast and the lunch specials are Chicken and Dumplings and Goulash."

"I should tell you, Wallace Singleton called. He said he was going to stop by sometime today to interview you. I tried to get him to stay away but you know Wallace."

"It wouldn't be so bad if he didn't publish his articles on his Facebook page. I know the event publicity is good for the town, but I just don't want Maggie exposed to it especially since she is so young."

Amy looked out the window and noticed Mr. Jeffers walking across the street.

"Better get the oatmeal going for Mr. Jeffers."

Amy held open the door for the elderly gentleman. "Good morning Mr. Jeffers."

"Ah, what's so good about 25 degrees and more snow," he grumbled.

"Come over here I have your coffee all ready, for you," Val said.

"Good morning, Mr. Jeffers," Maggie said as he sat down.

Val put his favorite coffee mug down on the counter in front of him. She poured herself a cup of coffee.

"Good morning, Maggie."

"My Mom won the blue ribbon."

"Good for her."

"Mr. Jeffers, do you know how to waltz? My teacher is going to show us how to do it. She said it is a very old dance, so I thought you would know how."

Val choked out her coffee. "Oh, excuse me."

Amy was trying not to laugh. "Would you like your usual breakfast today?"

Mr. Jeffers was a little taken aback "No, I'll have the French toast special." He puffed out his chest. "Yes, Maggie I know how to waltz."

"One French toast special coming up." Val headed to the backroom.

A few minutes later the song *Ten Minutes Ago* from Cinderella filled the diner airspace. Val was putting the topping on the French toast when Amy burst into the kitchen.

"You have got to come out here!"

Val picked up the platter and hurried into the main room. She almost dropped the plate when she saw Mr. Jeffers teaching Maggie to waltz. Maggie giggled, and Mr. Jeffers had a broad smile on his face. Amy picked up her phone to start filming this.

"No, Amy, this is their moment," Val said.

"Okay."

Val felt the tears well up in her eyes and she turned her head for just a moment, to regain her composure. She turned back around as Maggie giggled again. When the song ended Mr. Jeffers bowed, and Maggie bowed. Val laughed and walked over to her daughter.

"Thank you for the dance, Maggie."

"Thank you, Mr. Jeffers," Maggie replied.

"My darling daughter, I get to show you how to curtsey at the end of the waltz." Val did the proper curtsey. "Men bow and women curtsey."

"Oh, okay."

"Three years of dance school finally paid off."

"I used to be a dance instructor at the Arthur Murray dance studio." Mr. Jeffers sat down. "That is where I met my wife. She was a teacher there."

"I didn't know that," Val said.

"Well, that was a long time ago." Mr. Jeffers's tone suggested the topic was now closed.

Val glanced out the window and saw Wallace Singleton heading for her front door.

"Amy would you get Maggie some oatmeal and berries, and apple juice."

"I wanted the chocolate," Maggie protested.

"No chocolate for you today, you had enough sweets last night."

"Rats."

Amy handed her the oatmeal and then poured her a glass of apple juice.

Wallace opened the door, looking like he was straight out of Mayberry. Tall, skinny, comb-over black and gray hair. An old dark gray suit that he wore had seen many better days, along with a red bow tie.

"Good morning everyone."

"Hello, Wallace," Amy said.

"Good morning Val and everyone," James said as he opened the door and entered, Ben and Hal coming in behind him.

"Good morning, Gentleman. Wallace why don't you have a seat at one of the booths and Amy will be with you in just a moment." Val grabbed three menus and headed for the group of men. "Gentlemen, why don't you have a seat at one of the booths near the jukebox?"

They sat down at the table.

"Amy will be over in just a minute to get your orders." She handed them a menu and headed for the kitchen.

"Val," Wallace spoke as she walked by his table.

"I'm busy Wallace."

Ben leaned in towards the center of the table. "Why is Val acting so weird?"

"She hates reporters," Hal answered.

"Oh."

Amy walked over to the table. "Good morning. Do you all want coffee this morning?"

"Yes," they all answered together.

"What is good here this morning?" Hal asked.

"Well, Mr. Jeffers likes the French toast special."

"Really, I will have that then," Hal answered.

"Ben?"

"I'll take the sausage gravy and biscuits."

"James?"

"I'll take the corned beef hash special with the eggs over easy and wheat toast."

"Coming right up."

Val walked over to the counter and tapped Maggie on the shoulder.

"Missy you have ten minutes to finish up."

She walked into the kitchen and started working on the men's orders.

Amy carried four coffee mugs and the pot of coffee over to the table.

"Hal, I thought you and Rose were going Christmas shopping today."

"Yeah, we are heading down to Frederick. There is a Christmas store there that she wants to go to and then she wants to stop off at Happy Farms Restaurant combination general store on the way back."

"Is that the place that has the signs listing the menu along the side of the road?"

"Yeah, those signs start about two miles before you get to the restaurant," Amy added as she poured the coffee.

"They sell homemade apple butter and jams and jellies plus they have those heavy-duty sleeping bags there in the hunting section."

"Are you going hunting Hal?" James asked.

"We get a bunch of coats and a few sleeping bags for the Give Back Festival."

"What is that festival again?" James asked.

"Sort of like an angel tree like the Salvation Army has, but not exactly the same. Anyone in need can participate.

People can put their names on a tag for some sort of service they may need but can't afford. Some of our older people on fixed incomes may need some minor home repairs done or maybe someone to take them Christmas shopping. Of course, we try to provide Christmas for a lot of kids. People can put their own names on the tags or someone else can do it for them. Last year I was hurt, and I couldn't take down the Christmas decorations. Mayor Rob got our ticket and he and his family did that for us."

"Last year Amy and I bought clothes for the Ryan's, an elderly couple living on Maple Ave. We took their gift to them the Sunday before Christmas. We had so much fun. We check in on them about once every two weeks or so. Just to see if they need anything."

"Which reminds me we have to pick up yarn at the craft store today for Mrs. Ryan to make the Christmas scarves that she gives to everyone," Amy said as she turned and headed for the kitchen.

"Are there any tickets that don't get picked?" James asked.

"No, now some of us take a couple of tickets. It's about forming relationships with those in need and being there for them in the good times and the bad. I remember one family Rose and I helped. A single Mom with two kids and she was working full-time and trying to put herself through college. We helped with the Christmas presents and from time to time we watched her kids when work or school got too hectic. She graduated from school and is working at Johns Hopkins Hospital in Baltimore. She sends us emails and pictures of the kids. Her oldest boy is getting ready to graduate from high school next June and she already invited us to his graduation party."

"Wow. But what is the festive part of it." James asked.

"The Chamber of Commerce hired an orchestra to play some music and of course there is food. We have a great time."

"This is at the Chamber of Commerce building?"

"Yeah, we used to have it at the town ballroom. That is what we call it. It used to be a wedding reception type place. We used it for different festivals, parties and meetings."

"Why did you stop having it there?"

"Believe it or not that has been booked for weddings the past couple of years. People seem to want to get married this time of year."

A few minutes later, Amy returned balancing the plates of food on her tray.

"Okay, here we go gentlemen." She placed their orders in front of them. "Ben don't forget I get off at four today."

"Okay, I should be done by then."

Val walked out of the kitchen carrying Maggie's coat and backpack.

"Come on little one we have a bus to catch."

Maggie put her coat on and grabbed her backpack.

"If you don't mind," Mr. Jeffers started. "I would like to walk Maggie to the bus stop."

"I think that would be lovely," Val answered.

Mr. Jeffers pulled his wallet out from his back pocket.

"No, this is my treat today."

"You won't get rich that way."

"Seeing you dance with my daughter gave me a million-dollar smile today."

"You can't take that to the bank. Shall we go then Maggie?" He slid his walled back into his pocket.

"Yes, sir."

"Bye Mom."

"Bye Baby Girl."

Val watched them go out the door together as the Bakers walked in. Amy headed over toward Val.

"What got into him?"

"The kindness of a child."

Val swiveled toward the tables. She saw Wallace staring at his cup of coffee, and she took a deep sigh. She walked over to his booth and sat down in front of him.

"You got two minutes and you cannot use my full name and no pictures of me or Maggie. In fact, don't even mention Maggie. Those are my terms."

Wallace appeared a little taken aback as he grabbed his notebook from his pocket. "I am a little old fashioned; I still like to take notes instead of using my phone to record things."

"Come on Wallace, I got customers to feed."

"What was your inspiration for this year's display?"

"I found some antique toys when I had this place remodeled and I wanted to put them to good use, so Santa's workshop seemed like the perfect fit."

"Who designed the painting?"

"My employee, Chris."

"So where is your blue ribbon?"

"In my office."

"Any plans to put it on display?"

"No."

"Why not?"

"It is not my style."

"Bragging?"

"I just prefer to keep my successes quiet. This year I won, next year it may be someone else's turn. It is all good fun."

"Well, it won't be Betsy next year."

"What do you mean?" Val asked.

"She is putting the shop up for sale after the first of the year. She wants to retire."

"I didn't know that. Wow, well I wish her all the best and your two minutes are up."

"You know I am not like those other reporters."

"I know that, but you have a Facebook page and a following. I am not willing to put my or my daughter's face out there. Now, are you going to respect my terms?"

"Of course."

"Okay then." Val got up from the table and turned toward the counter. "Amy, please give Wallace a cinnamon roll." She turned and looked at him. "No charge." Val headed for the kitchen.

The door opened and the Bakers walked in. They sat down in one of the booths near the counter.

Amy walked to the "men's table with a pot of coffee.

"Who needs a refill?"

"I do," all three of them answered, at the same time.

"So, I guess Val is going to let Wallace write a story about her?" James asked.

"Not really, it is about the festival and her winning last night, but no pictures of her or Maggie and no listing of their last names."

"It is a miracle no one has posted or mentioned her already," James said.

"We respect each other here," Hal answered.

"Yeah, but what about the tourists?"

"Most are too busy to notice or if they do post it, anything hasn't caught on yet."

"What happens when it does come out?" Ben asked.

"Hopefully the sky won't fall. She has been through enough."

"I better get Wallace's roll and the Bakers look like they are ready to order." She turned and headed for the counter area.

"My Dad okayed using his story" Ben said.

"What?"

"What we talked about at the pub, remember?"

"Oh yeah, tell him I said thank you."

Chapter Eleven

Thomas walked through the diner backdoor at precisely 2:15 p.m. Val was sitting in her office when she heard the door close. She got up from her desk and headed for the kitchen.

"Good afternoon, Thomas. How are things?"

"Fine ma'am."

"I saved a bowl of goulash for you. Go hang up your coat, and after you eat you can start on the dishes."

"Thank you, ma'am."

"Before I forget, in my office there is a tin of sugar cookies for your family and some apple butter."

"You didn't have to do that ma'am."

"I can't take the credit for that one, Ms. Rose brought them by."

"Now let's get moving, there are a lot of dishes to get done."

Val headed for the dining area. As she walked through the door, she saw James closing the front door behind him, and she smiled as she walked toward him.

"Twice in one day. To what do I owe the pleasure?"

"I hear you have excellent chili and I had about all my ears could take of the handbell festival. Don't get me wrong it is lovely, but…"

"It is not your kind of thing. Why don't you hang up your coat and do you want a salad to go with that?"

"Yes, with the Catalina dressing."

"Okay, you just missed the lunch crowd, and the dinner crowd starts around five." She walked beside him. "I know what you mean about the handbell festival. I tried going last year and left shortly after it started."

"Why?" James sat down on one of the counter stools.

"I have a five-year-old, who just wasn't ready for that type of culture just yet."

"So, will you try again?"

"Maybe when Maggie is about thirty."

"That bad?"

"Yeah."

"Where is Amy?"

"She had a Christmas errand to run. Chris will be here any minute and then I have to go watch Maggie at the play practice."

"Sounds like a busy afternoon."

"I am a single Mom, so every day is busy." She turned and headed for the kitchen. Once on the other side, she stopped to compose herself. *What am I doing?*

Thomas looked up from the sink.

"Are you okay ma'am?'

"Yes, why?"

"Your face is turning red."

"It's just a little too warm in here."

Val sat in the next to the last pew at the church and watched as the junior choir director tried to wrangle up all the children in the play and get them to stand in their places. Val snickered under her breath.

"Trying to get youngsters to stay in one place for longer than a minute is as easy as trying to put socks on a cat."

Val jumped at the sound of someone behind her. She turned around and saw Betsy.

"Betsy, I didn't hear you come in. Is one of your grandchildren in the play this year?"

"Yes, Abby, the last angel on the left." She pointed to her granddaughter.

"That's Abby? She's getting so big; I didn't recognize her."

"Yes, my daughter is minding the store, so I can steal a few minutes away," Betsy answered.

"Is it true you are selling the place?"

"Yes,"

"Do you mind, if I ask why?"

"I started working at that store when my parents owned it. I was just fifteen years old. After my husband and I got divorced, I raised my three children in the apartment above the store. To tell the truth, I am just tired of it all. A few years ago, I made myself a promise that when my youngest graduated from college and got settled I would sell the place and move to Florida."

"How long ago was that?"

"It took nine years, my youngest took a while in that getting settled department. But he is now working for a law firm."

"So, are you still moving to Florida?"

"The love of grandchildren is keeping me here."

"What about your daughter taking over the store?"

"Oh, no. She has made it clear that she just wants to be a full-time mom."

The children started singing *Away in a Manager* loudly. Val and Betsy turned toward them.

Betsy watched Val for a moment.

"Wallace wants to retire from the newspaper," Betsy added.

"I didn't know that."

"Yeah, he is trying to find someone to take it over."

"Wait! Are you and Wallace?"

"No, we're only good friends, since high school."

"Well, hopefully he will find someone."

"By the way, a secret elf left me a Christmas present at my back door this morning. Would you know anything about that?"

"There are a lot of secret elves in Festive this time of year."

"That wasn't a no."

"It wasn't a yes either."

"Val, life has dealt the both of us a tough hand. But sometimes we get the chance to reshuffle the deck."

Val looked at her hands

"That is just a thought my dear." Betsy finished.

"Mommy," Maggie yelled. "Listen to me sing."

"Okay, honey."

Chris walked into the diner and immediately noticed James sitting at the counter. He grimaced as he hung his jacket and scarf on the coat rack. Amy appeared from the back room carrying a slice of Lemon Cream pie. She placed the pie on the counter in front of James.

"More coffee?" she asked.

"Yes please."

"Is it always this quiet during the late afternoon here?"

"No, most of the time a lot of locals are here getting an early dinner or gossiping over a cup of coffee. A lot of people volunteer for the Frosty Festival, so I guess they are at the park now setting things up."

"What happens at the Frosty Festival?"

"They make an outdoor skating rink. They put up a little house for Santa and Frosty where kids can have their pictures taken with one of them or both. They have booths for people to sell homemade crafts. There is a makeshift barn area where the reindeer are kept."

"Reindeer?"

"Oh yeah, one of the local farmers raises reindeer, they have sleigh rides, with reindeer pulling the sleds."

"He makes a living from having reindeer?"

"I guess there is a market for reindeer meat. Plus, the ones he uses for the sleigh rides also have been used in a couple of Christmas movies."

Chris walked over toward Amy.

"Hi Chris, I was just telling James about the Frosty Festival."

"That means we will be very busy Saturday, with all of the tourists in town," Chris said.

"Don't remind me, Last year I don't think I had a chance to breathe the entire day. Plus, with all of the tourists there won't be a lot of parking spaces around."

"I forget when the Give Back Festival is." James asked.

"That is on Saturday night."

Chris looked at his watch "Amy, don't you have to meet Ben in a few minutes?"

"Oh, I lost track of the time. I have to go."

"What does my check come to?"

"Ten dollars and fifty cents."

"Okay," James pulled his wallet out of his pocket and left a five-dollar bill for a tip.

"Chris, can you ring up James ticket, I have got to move." Amy grabbed her purse from under the counter. "I don't mean to be rude, but thanks and have a good evening." She headed for the front door and grabbed her coat just before she headed outside.

James got up and walked over to the cash register to pay the bill. Chris rang up his bill with a tough scowl on his face.

"Chris, if I was a betting man, I would wager that you don't like me very much."

"I don't know you, but I think you are hiding something from Val."

James looked at him for a moment. "What makes you think that?"

"Instinct."

"Instincts can be wrong."

"Maybe, but I don't think so."

"Have a good evening." James headed toward the door.

When he reached his car, James paused for a moment and looked at the diner's Christmas window. He smiled and then he frowned.

"He is right, I am hiding something," he whispered.

Val gathered up the grocery bags from the back of the van, and Maggie followed her to their front door. She unlocked the door and they walked inside.

"Maggie, go hang up your coat and get started on your homework while I cook dinner."

"What's for dinner?"

"Vegetable soup and a turkey sandwich."

"Yum."

"Okay girl, get moving, I have to bake cookies tonight."

Val started putting the groceries away and her phone rang. She looked at the caller id and saw Roses number.

"Hi Rose, how are you?"

"I am fine. How was your day?"

"Busy."

"I won't keep you long. Do you have a recipe for a cranberry Christmas cake?"

"With or without brandy?"

"Without."

"I can email you a recipe later this evening. Do you have a special event going on?"

"Ben has asked for my help; Saturday is his and Amy's anniversary of their very first date and he wants to surprise her with her favorite cake."

"Okay, do you think he is going to propose?"

"Have mercy, I hope so. I guess you heard the rumor that Betsy is putting her store up for sale."

"No rumor, it is true, I saw her at play practice this afternoon."

"Why? She is busy as ever."

"She wants to retire and so does Wallace."

"You don't say, Wow!"

"Mommy, I can't find my crayons," Maggie yelled from her room.

"I need to go."

"Have a good night."

"Goodnight." She hung up the phone "Look in your backpack, Maggie."

After dinner was finished at the inn, James walked into the living room. He grabbed a log from the basket on the hearth and knelt down on the floor as he placed the wood on the fire, and then stared at the flame while it began burning.

He heard footsteps approaching, and when he glanced over, he saw Hal coming into the room.

"A good fire can be good therapy," Hal said.

"How so?"

"Well, it gives you something else to concentrate on for a moment or two. And it's good for a man to sit in front of a fire every now and then, just reflecting on what needs to be done or counting his many blessings."

"I guess so." James got up and walked over toward one of the chairs and sat down, "Where is Rose?" he asked.

"Upstairs setting up one of the rooms. We have a family coming in tomorrow from Arizona. They love the Frosty Festival with all of the snow" Hal sat down in the chair closest to James.

"What if it doesn't snow?"

"We have snow making machines just in case."

"I see."

"James, this may be none of my business, but you seem to be a man with something on his mind this evening."

"Yeah," James leaned over in Hal's direction. "You know that I am a reporter and that I am here to cover the festivities during the holidays, right?"

"Right."

"Well, I am rather fond of Val, and given her feeling toward reporters…"

"Yes, go on."

"I haven't told her that I'm a reporter."

"Oh no!"

"Plus, my boss wants me to do a story on her."

"How did he find out she was here?"

"I sent him a picture of the wedding photo on Val's desk" James paused, took a deep breath and let it out, then spoke again.

"Basically, he is demanding I do the story. I have been stalling, but he is getting impatient. I could lose my job and I really like Val and Maggie."

"As I see it you have three choices. One; you could say nothing and hope it doesn't come out. But we both know that won't work. I am surprised that the truth hasn't come out already with all of the tourists we have in town and social media."

"What is my second choice?"

"Tell Val the truth and try to repair any damage that may happen."

"My third choice?"

"Tell Val the truth, don't write the story and quit your job."

"Well, not working is not really an option right now; I help my mother with her bills."

"I suggest you have a conversation with your mother about the finances first then tell Val as soon as possible. If she finds out from someone else, she may not forgive you for not being truthful with her."

James looked down at his hands.

"I think you'll make the right decision." Hal got up, "I better go check on Rose and see if she needs anything."

James continued looking over at the fire, staring at the flames, a frown pulling his brows.

Val was putting away the last of the dinner dishes and gave a long glance over at Maggie. She caught the intense look of concentration Maggie was giving her drawing. Val put the plates in the cabinet and then quietly walked over to stand by her daughter.

"What are you working on?"

"It is a picture of you at the diner."

"Of me?"

"Yeah, there, see?" Maggie picked up the drawing and started pointing to each character. "There is Amy, and there is the silver counter."

"The one with the red hair."

"That's you carrying a plate of food."

"Who is the person with the hat on?"

"That is Mr. Jeffers."

"So, I guess you are the one with all the long brown curly hair, standing next to Mr. Jeffers."

"That's me."

"Did you have fun today, when Mr. Jeffers was showing you how to dance?"

"Yes," Maggie let out a sigh.

"Okay, I know that sigh, what is on your mind."

"Did my Daddy like to dance?"

Val swallowed hard and looked down at her hands for a moment.

"Yes, he did."

"Was he good at it?"

"He tried hard."

"Do you like to dance, Mama?"

Val smiled, and she got up. "You wait right here; I'll be right back." She turned and walked toward her bedroom.

A few minutes later Val emerged with her boom box and a CD.

"Come on, get up Maggie. Let's dance." She put the CD in the player

"Do we have to waltz?"

"No, we will freestyle it."

Pink's song *Good Old Days* filled the air.

"Come on; just move side to side like me."

Maggie followed along.

"That's it, you got it."

Maggie giggled.

About an hour later the phone rang. Val glanced at the caller id number.

"Hey, Chris, how are things at the diner?"

"We are just getting ready to close up for the night."

"Were you busy?"

"We had a little bit of a dinner rush but nothing that we couldn't handle. Some of the members of the Baltimore Handbell choir stayed after the competition and they stopped in for dinner. Thomas came back after his regular shift wanting to pick up some extra time. So, I let him work two hours. I didn't think you would mind, and I needed the help."

"That is fine. I just worry about his grades slipping with all of the time he is putting in at the diner."

"I guess he just wants this to be a good Christmas for his family."

"Did he tell you that?"

"His Mom is working a lot. And with his Dad gone."

"Rose and I are working on a few things for them. What about the Give Back Festival?"

"I think he is a little too proud for that."

"Okay, you just gave me an idea."

"Oh, boy."

"Leave a reminder on my desk to call the toy store and Robertson's clothing store tomorrow morning. Also, leave a note for everyone that I am opening up the employee Christmas party to family members this year."

"Done."

"Now I have to get Maggie in bed and bake cookies for her class Christmas party tomorrow."

"You also need to order more Orange Soda and cheddar cheese."

"Put that on the note."

"Got it. Goodnight boss."

"Goodnight."

James sat in front of his computer in his room working on the next installment for the paper. He started proofreading the article when an email message popped up on his screen. He opened the email from his boss and read.

"When are you going to send the story on Val Young? The work you have been sending in has been fine for the style page. However, if you want to get back on the front page you need to get this story or start looking for another job."

"Jerk," James whispered. He went back to proofreading the article on the handbell choirs. "Perfect," he muttered.

He attached the article and accompanying pictures to his bosses' email. Along with one extra line he typed in. "Working on it."

James closed his computer, picked up his phone, and punched in his mother's phone number.

"Hello," she answered.

"Hi, Mom,"

"Hi James, Everybody, James is on the phone, how are you son? I tell you Thelma, Gladys and Harvey are here. We are playing cribbage, and I got a meat and cheese tray from the deli and Thelma brought a chocolate éclair cake. Harvey supplied a blackberry wine. I never knew they made blackberry wine. Did you lose your gloves again? James, are you still there?"

"Yeah, Mom, I am still here."

"We were just talking about your stories and we all love them. When are you coming home?"

"Probably Christmas Eve," James sighed.

"What's wrong?"

"Nothing's wrong, Mom."

"You sighed; something is wrong. I'm your mother I know when something is going on."

"Nothing is wrong, Mom, I promise. I'm just checking in to see how you are doing. Why don't you get back to your guests and I'll call you tomorrow?"

"You swear nothing is wrong?"

"I swear."

"All right then."

"Goodnight Mom."

"Goodnight."

At the moment his Mom hung up the phone he heard her whisper, "He's in love and he won't tell me." When the line went dead, he fully realized his Mom was right.

At 8:00 a.m. the next morning, James walked into the dinner, cast a searching glance around the room looking for Val and did not see her. But he did notice Rose and Hal sitting at one of the tables. Maggie was sitting next to Mr. Jeffers. She was eating pancakes and Mr. Jeffers was having bacon and eggs. The Mayor and his wife were seated at a table near the jukebox. He walked over to his usual spot. Amy appeared from the back carrying a platter of food.

"James, I will be with you in just a moment."

"That's fine, Good morning everyone." He said as he took a seat.

"Hello," Maggie said.

"Maggie where is your Mom?"

"She's in the back cooking," she answered.

Amy strolled over to the counter. "Our specials this morning are strawberry bliss omelet, blueberry almond crepes, or French toast with maple sausage. What can I get for you this morning?"

"I will try the strawberry bliss omelet with a side of bacon, and a coffee."

"Coming right up."

"Amy, you seem a little bit rushed today?"

She stopped for a moment. "I am just mad at Ben, that's all. He is in the doghouse now. He was supposed to pick me up after work today, so we could go Christmas shopping, but he forgot and made other plans to go out with his friends. We'll go tomorrow, he said. Like I don't have other plans."

"Oh," James said as he looked down at the counter, lost for any reply to her rant.

"Men!" Amy mumbled and put his mug of coffee on the counter in front of him, then headed for the backroom.

"You had to ask her?" Mr. Jeffers said.

A few minutes later Val walked into the room carrying James breakfast.

"Good morning, James, Amy is taking a short break." She put the food down on the counter.

"Val, I need to talk to you."

"Can it wait? I have to meet with Rose and Hal and then I have some other things to do today."

"Yeah."

"Okay then."

"Maggie you have only five minutes to finish up."

Val walked over to Rose and Hal's table and sat down

"So, what is this secret mission you need help with?" Rose asked.

"Thomas and his family."

"How can we help?" Hal asked.

"I need you to play Santa Claus."

"You mean wear the red suit and the beard thing?"

"Yes, I do."

"I need you to be here at my employee Christmas party."

"What are you up to?" Rose asked.

"I am inviting the families to the party this year. When Thomas' brothers and sisters sit on Santa's lap, you get a list of the Christmas presents they want, then Rose will text the manager at the toy store and the clothing store to get the gifts together. One of Santa's helpers will deliver the gifts Christmas Eve."

"Who gets to play the elf?"

"I am working on that one."

"Deal."

"What has you so busy today?"

"Maggie's school party is today, and she volunteered me to help out and I have Christmas errands to run. Plus, it's my turn to take dinner over to Carrie's house. Her Dad is still in the hospital,"

"You're a busy woman," Hal stated.

"Speaking of busy, Maggie go get your coat on and your boots."

"Yes, ma'am" Maggie slid off the stool.

Amy walked back into the room. She refilled James coffee mug.

"Hal, go say hello to the Mayor for a minute."

"Why am I going to do that?"

"Amy needs some girl time, now scoot."

"All right," Hal got up and walked toward the Mayor's table.

"Amy, come over here."

She walked over to Rose. "Do you need more coffee?"

"I need you to sit down and tell me what is really wrong."

Amy sat down, quiet for a moment, and then mumbled. "Ben and I were supposed to go shopping for his presents for his parents."

"And what else?" Rose asked.

"He forgot and made plans with his friends."

"And what else is going on?"

Amy looked down at the table for a long moment, pushing a crumb around in a figure eight with her fingertip.

"I have something important I want to talk to him about."

"Does he know that?"

"No."

"So, I have a little advice for you. Tonight, call some of your girlfriends and have a girl's night out. Remember that occasionally, a man needs to get together with his friends, so you go have fun too. Important discussions need to take place in privacy, and not while shopping. Okay?"

"Okay."

"Now go call Ben."

"I will."

Maggie skipped along beside her Mom up Main Street. Maggie had the advent calendar gift in her hand.

"So, who gets the surprise today?" Val asked.

Maggie pointed to a car. "That one."

Val smiled. "Okay, let's go slide the envelope under the windshield wipers, and then we have to hurry to the bus stop."

Twenty minutes later James emerged from the diner. As he headed towards his car, he spied a red envelope under the windshield wiper. He lifted the wiper blade and took the item out. He opened the envelope and pulled out the Christmas card. On the front of the card was a cartoon picture of a reindeer dressed in a red sweater. The inside of the card read 'May your Holidays be filled with warmth and cheer.' There was a credit card sized gift card inside for the shell gas station. The card was signed Santa's elves.

"Elves come in all shapes and sizes" he whispered and got in the car.

James parked his car in the hotel parking lot, picked up the gift card and frowned. He looked at it for a moment and then opened the glove box and put the card inside. Looking across the yard he noticed Hal standing at the woodpile. James got out of his car closed the door and headed toward Hal.

"Can I help you with that?" James asked.

"Sure, it's supposed to get down into the teens tonight. I thought I should bring in some extra firewood."

"That sounds like a plan."

Hal noticed the troubled looked on James' face. "You haven't told her yet."

"No, I wanted to speak with her this morning, but she was so busy at the diner."

"The diner is not the place to have that discussion. You must talk to her someplace private. That way she is free to react the way she needs to."

"Which means chew me out."

"Maybe, but to some extent you deserve that for not telling her the truth from the get-go. The longer you wait the more you risk her finding out from someone else."

"I didn't want to hurt her."

"That's only an excuse you are telling yourself. Trust me, I know. I almost lost my Rosie when I was in a similar situation. I waited, and she found out the truth from someone else. It took months before she would trust me again."

"I get your point."

"Now enough of the lecture. Let's get this wood inside."

Side-by-side they went to the building, then entered just as Rose came into the lobby carrying a plate full of cookies.

"Well, you just missed Val. She dropped off an order of cookies for tomorrow night and of course she brought some extra ones. The white ones are anisette cookies, the round brown ones are some sort of French cookies, and the ones with the jam are German Spitzbuben cookies. I may not be able to pronounce all of the names right, but I sure love to eat them."

"Me too," Hal exclaimed his eyes sparkling over like a kid on Christmas Eve.

"You're worse than a kid in the toy store." Rose teased. "Save some for our guests."

"Rats."

"Where are the Bakers?" James asked.

"They went to the Tea Room. That is a little place near the movie theater that sells specialty teas from all over the world and they make cucumber sandwiches. Come to think of it, Val just loves their Christmas tea blend."

"I got the hint. But I will be leaving before Christmas."

"Well, you don't have to wait till Christmas to give her a gift. She also likes Swiss Chocolates."

"Where can I get those?"

"Betsy's"

"I need to get some work done," James said.

"Okay then. Before I forget, we are having a dinner here this evening for one of our guests. If you would like to attend; dinner will be at seven."

"Thank you." James headed up the stairs.

"He has it bad for Val," Rose spoke quietly, and then smiled.

"I just hope he doesn't blow it," Hal whispered as Rose turned to walk out of the room.

Before noon Val stumbled into the back of the diner from the parking lot, carrying several bags from the local toy store and the children's clothing store. She saw Chris was busy at the grill making hamburgers.

"Boss, you need some help there?" Chris asked.

"No thanks, I have to hide these in the storeroom, so Maggie doesn't see them. Plus, I have some other bags in the van for Hal and Rose."

Val walked into the storeroom and she placed the bags on one of the shelves. "Whew, I am tired already," Val said as she went back into the kitchen and looked around the room. "Where is Amy?"

"Out front talking to Ben."

"Did they patch things up?"

"I hope so," Chris replied.

"Okay, I'm heading back out to my van."

Chris put a burger and fries on a plate and rang the bell. "Orders up, Amy."

A few minutes later as Val was putting the last of the bags on the storeroom shelf, Amy walked into the room.

"Hi, how did the rest of the morning go?" Val asked.

"Oh, the usual, not too busy," Amy answered.

"Did you make up with Ben?"

"Yes, and tonight I am going out with some of my girlfriends. We are getting our nails done and going shopping for some new outfits for ourselves."

"Sounds like a plan."

"I'm thinking about getting that purple dress that is in the display window at Carmen's shop."

"The one with the silver trim around the neck and sleeves, or the one with the silver belt?"

"The one with the trim."

"That is a good choice."

"Why don't you come with us? Maybe Rose could babysit."

"Thank you for the invite, but Rose has a big dinner to cook for tonight, so I have got to work here tonight"

Amy looked at the floor. "Oh."

"I tell you what, how about you and I go out to the tea shop on Monday. Since we are closed and then we can head over to the jewelry store and get some bling to go with that dress."

Amy smiled. "Yes, ma'am. One can never have enough bling. That's my motto."

Around seven that evening, Val emerged from the kitchen area. The dinner rush had finally calmed down and Chris and Maggie were sitting at the counter. Chris was helping her with her spelling assignment.

"Spell apple," Chris asked.

"A p p l e."

"Good one, now spell snow."

"S n o w."

"Okay, now here is a tough one, banana."

"b a n n – no, one n. How many ns are there Mama?"

"You tell me," Val answered as she walked toward them.

Maggie sighed. "B a n n a n a."

"No." Chris replied.

"Rats," Maggie snapped her fingers.

"Try again," Val said.

"Oh, all right, b a n a n a."

"Right on." Chris smiled.

"Maggie, you need to go get your backpack and coat out of my office because we will be leaving soon."

"Yes, ma'am." She slid off the stool and headed toward the door.

"Wait a minute." Maggie stopped. "What do you say to Chris?"

"Thank you for helping me with my spelling words."

"You're welcome." Chris smiled and watched Maggie heading for the office.

"She is something else," Chris said as he turned and started to clear away some dishes from the counter.

"Yes, she is," Val ran her fingers across the counter. "But I worry about her not having her Dad or a Grandfather around."

"Was your Dad around when you were growing up?"

"No, he left when I was a baby."

"You turned out okay. You know there is nothing Hal, or I wouldn't do for her. To me, she is my adopted niece. I already have her Christmas present picked out."

"Thank you for saying that."

"Not just words, I mean it."

"I know you do."

"All right then."

"You and Thomas close up shop at eight, and could you give Thomas a ride home?"

"Sure."

"There are a few slices of sugar cream pie left in the fridge, so why don't you take those and give the left-over chili to Thomas."

"Okay Boss," Chris continued to wipe down the counter.

"Wait a minute."

Chris stopped cleaning.

"Tell me that you did not get my daughter a puppy." Val tilted her head to the side.

"I did not get her a puppy."

Val sighed in relief.

"I got her a kitten."

"What?" Val snapped.

"Just kidding, Boss."

"Ha, ha," Val sarcastically answered.

James walked into the living room. He noticed that Rose had set a coffee tray on one of the tables and he poured himself a cup of coffee. He took a few sips and stared at the fireplace. Hal stepped into the room.

"Guess it is time to put another log on the fire," Hal said.

"I was just thinking about that."

"No, you were not, you were thinking about our previous discussion." Hal walked toward the fireplace and leaned over to pull a log out of the basket.

"Busted, here let me get that." James put his cup down on the mantle and reached for the log.

"I guess you had enough discussion of geology from our two professors," Hal whispered.

"They lost me somewhere around the geological finds in Brazil's Xingo Canyons," James said as he settled the log on the fire.

"You hung in there longer than I did. When I was growing up the men in my family usually talked about sports and work during dinner."

"That hasn't changed much except that the discussions now are about fantasy football, work and video games."

For a long moment, James gazed at the fire then spoke again "I am supposed to take Val to the movie festival tomorrow. I thought about telling her then, but. Maggie will be with us."

"That is not a good time to tell to have a serious conversation on confessing the truth."

"I know."

"She will be busy since the Frosty Festival is Saturday. Maybe you should try for Sunday after church. The Tea Room is open on Sunday. They have a small private room you can reserve. If I remember right, there was something in the church newsletter about the kids having play practice on Sunday."

"That sounds like a good idea."

Val was about halfway home when she looked into the rear-view mirror and saw Maggie staring out the window of the van.

"Tell me something you learned today in school."

"My teacher asked us what we want to be when we grow up."

"What did you tell her?"

"I don't know, I'm only five."

"Well you could be … What a minute is that what you told her?"

"Yes. She got mad when everyone laughed."

"Is there a note from your teacher that I have to sign?"

"No."

"Okay."

"There are two slips."

"What is the other one for?"

"The trip to the reindeer farm."

"Child, you definitely have my personality."

"Am I in trouble?"

"Did you lie?"

"No, ma'am."

"Then you are not in trouble with me. And if your teacher is upset, I will take care of things with her. Have you finished all of your homework?"

"Yes, ma'am."

"Then you can watch television for half an hour then off to bed."

"Okay."

Rich, she has your looks, but she has my sassiness, she thought. Val made the left turn into the driveway.

Val unlocked the door and they walked into the living room. Maggie zipped open her backpack and handed Val the notes. She sat down on the couch and reached for the remote.

"Excuse me child, where do your backpack and your coat belong?"

Maggie let out a heavy sigh as she got up from the couch and gathered her belongings and headed for her room.

She has my sassy side.

Chapter Twelve

Rose walked into the diner a little after 8:00 a.m. She saw Maggie sitting next to Mr. Jeffers. Maggie let out a giggle. Amy was busy with some other customers, so Rose sat down in one of the booths. Val walked into the room from the kitchen carrying two plates of food.

"Here is your egg and cheese omelet, Mr. Jeffers, and one strawberry bliss omelet for you, pumpkin."

"Thank you," Maggie said.

"Eat up, because you have only fifteen minutes before the bus."

"Yes, ma'am."

Val looked up and noticed Rose sitting in one of the booths. She grabbed a menu from the cash register area and headed over.

"Good morning, Rose. How are you this morning?" Val handed her a menu.

"I am fine, I won't need a menu, I already heard you have those strawberry omelets today. So, I will have that with a side of bacon and coffee."

"Who told you I have the omelet special today?"

"Ben called this morning; he is helping Hal with a project. We are thinking about buying the three-bedroom house next to our place and we can rent that place out to small families." Rose paused to take a long breath then spoke again. "Hal and Ben are going to look at it today. Ben is going to give him an estimate on what would cost to fix it up."

"Well that is a good approach to take, do you have a minute?" Val said.

"Of course."

Val sat down across from Rose. "What do you know about Ms. Ellis?"

Rose let out a groan. "Ms. Ellis was my son's first-grade teacher, and she told me that my son would never amount to anything."

"Your son is an engineer for NASA, right?'

"Yeah, she said the same thing about our daughter."

"Your daughter is an attorney."

"Okay, so why are you asking?"

"Ms. Ellis sent a note home yesterday, she said my daughter refused to follow her instructions and did not answer the question concerning what she wanted to be when she grows up. When she said, "I don't know I am only five," that action caused a disruption in her class and I need to teach my daughter to follow directions, so there will be no future problems."

"What did you write on that note?"

"I told her that my daughter was following my instructions concerning telling the truth and if she does not know the answer to a question to admit that. Also, if Ms. Ellis has a problem with how I am raising my daughter that I would be happy to meet with her and the principal as soon as possible."

"Good for you, that woman does not belong in a classroom."

"Well, I will have your order out in just a few minutes." She got up to leave.

"Wait a minute, did Ben and Amy make up?" Rose asked.

"Yes, and check out Amy's nails. She has Santa Claus's hat painted on each one of them."

"It seems she took my advice."

"That she did."

Val looked up when she heard the front door open. She noticed James rushing in and shaking the snow off his coat.

"It is freezing cold out there," he said.

Val walked away from the table and took his coat. "Here, I can hang that up for you, why don't you go sit at the counter and I'll get you a cup of coffee."

James noticed Rose sitting at the booth "Good morning Rose, may I join you?"

"Of course," Rose answered.

Val smiled. "All right then, while I am getting your coffee our specials today are, Strawberry bliss omelet, waffles with blueberries and our cranberry crepes with scrapple. Plus, all specials come with a side of scrapple."

"What a minute, Ben didn't tell me you had crepes today."

"Do you want to change your order?"

"Wait, nah."

"Okay. I will be right back coffee for both of you." Val headed for the counter.

James looked at his hands for a moment.

"Hal already told me about your problem."

"I know I should have told her sooner, but I really care about her and Maggie."

"I was a little surprised that you hadn't told her already."

"Do you have any advice?"

"Be gentle with the truth and don't be surprised if she gets very angry."

"Okay," James sighed.

Rose looked up and saw Val heading for their table. "So, are you going to the movie festival tonight?" Rose asked in an obvious attempt to change the subject.

Val walked over and put a mug down in front of James. "What would you like today?" Then put Rose's coffee in front of her.

"I will take the crepes, but what is scrapple?"

"A local breakfast meat trust me you will love it," Rose answered.

"Okay then, I will try the scrapple."

"Two specials coming right up." Val turned and headed for the kitchen, but as she approached the counter area she looked over and saw Mr. Jeffers's coffee mug was almost empty. She walked behind the counter and grabbed the coffee pot. "How about a refill?"

"Just half a cup," he answered.

"Are you going to the movies tonight?" Maggie asked.

"Yes," he answered.

"My Mom and Mr. James are taking me to see White Christmas."

"I am going to see *It's a Wonderful Life.*"

"Can we see that too, Mama?"

"Not this time, that movie runs way past your bedtime."

"Rats."

A few minutes later Val emerged from the kitchen area carrying Rose and James' breakfast specials.

"Here you go, a strawberry bliss omelet and cranberry crepes." She put the plates down on the table.

"I was just telling James about your famous pulled beef sandwiches, last year the line was out the door. People were waiting to get in here." Rose said.

"Tell me about it. I got the beef marinating right now. I also have the apples simmering for my homemade applesauce."

"That sounds good," James said.

"What are your other specials tomorrow so I can let Hal know?"

"Breakfast specials are buttermilk pancakes, sausage and gravy. Lunch specials are the pulled beef sandwiches, vegetable soup with salad and chicken pot pie. I almost forgot I have a red velvet cake and lemon Chiffon pie also. I'm keeping it simple this year. We will be closing at five tomorrow. That way I can take Maggie to visit Santa Claus."

"I know Hal will get the red velvet cake. Is Maggie still asking for a puppy?" Rose whispered.

"I hope not." Val turned to leave.

"Val," James started. "Can you text me your address?"

"Of course, Maggie is very excited about the movie."

"I will be there to pick you up at six on the dot then."

Val walked away as Rose looked directly at James.

"Sunday," He lowered his eyes "I will tell her on Sunday."

At 4:30 p.m. Val opened the door to the log cabin and immediately switched on the outside Christmas lights. She noticed Maggie was not walking in behind her. Looking outside she saw her daughter standing in the middle of their yard staring at the house across the street.

"Look Ma, they have real deer in their yard."

Val went back out where her daughter was standing and looked across the street. Two does and one enormous buck with a full set of antlers were chewing on some of the neighbor's bushes. She smiled at the magic for just a moment. "They are beautiful, but we have to get ready for tonight."

"Can I pet the deer?" Maggie asked.

"No honey, those are wild animals and they should not get used to us humans."

"Oh, all right," Maggie sighed.

"This morning, I put your snowflake sweatshirt and blue jeans on your bed, so while I am getting a shower you change your clothes."

Val opened the front door, held it for Maggie then closed it behind them.

"Mom, when are we putting up our inside tree?"

"On Sunday after we get home from play practice."

"Oh, okay."

"While I am getting my shower, you can get started on your homework, so it is done."

"Can we get pizza for dinner?"

"Yes, you can get a slice of pizza at the movie theater. Now go get ready."

"Yes, ma'am"

At 5:00 p.m. James walked into the lobby of the movie theater. He carried his camera into the building. The lobby was already filled with parents and children. The old-fashioned theater floor was covered with a red carpet, and there were crystal chandeliers hanging from the ceiling. A few gold ornate vintage sofas lined the walls. To the right of the entrance door were the wooden ticket desk and the snack bar area.

"I wonder if they have a balcony," he said out loud.

"They do," Ben said as he walked up behind him.

"Ben, I didn't see you when I walked in."

"I was over there by the corn-hole game. Toss three bags into the hole and win a free popcorn."

"How did you do?"

"I got two."

"I thought I would take some pictures and get tickets for White Christmas before picking up Val and Maggie."

"Yeah, I am getting tickets for me and Amy too. There are a couple of those photo boards that people put their faces in and get a picture taken over by the theater entrance. They got Santa and Mrs. Claus. The Grinch with Cindy Lou Who and Max. Oh yeah, they have the elves from Rudolph too."

"Thanks for letting me know." James turned to walk away.

"James," Ben started. "You can get a pizza deal with your tickets."

"I don't know what Maggie and Val would like."

"Just get the deal now and you can order when you all get here. Trust me; they have the best pizza in town."

"Okay, Thanks for the info." Ben walked away.

James surveyed the room as he lifted the camera to his face focused and started taking pictures.

A few minutes before six Val walked into the living room carrying hers and Maggie's coats and gloves. Maggie was sitting on the floor playing with one of her dolls.

"Maggie, James is going to be here any minute. So, is your homework done?"

"Yes, ma'am."

"Did you give the notes to your teacher, Ms. Ellis?"

"Yes, ma'am."

"Did she say anything about what I wrote to her?"

"No, ma'am. She just turned all red and told me to go back to my desk."

Did she now. Val smiled. "Don't let me forget the bags I put in the kitchen. They are for our secret elf mission tonight."

"Okay, Momma does that mean Mr. James is a secret elf too?"

"He is one just for tonight."

"Okay."

Val heard a car pull into the driveway. "He is here. Remember to be on your best behavior tonight, Maggie Sue."

"Got it Mom." Val raised one eyebrow. "I mean yes ma'am."

"That's better."

A bit nervous, Val jumped a little when a knock sounded on the door. She took a deep breath and opened the door and saw James standing there wearing a camel color coat with snow gathering on his shoulders and hair. *Breathe.*

"Hi, come on in."

James looked at Val for just a second before stepping inside. "You look amazing." He said.

"Oh, thank you. I just threw on some jeans and a sweater." Val felt her face grow warm from blushing and hoped he did not notice. "We are supposed to get a couple of inches of snow tonight."

"Yeah it's really coming down out there already, so we should get going."

"Maggie, come on, get your coat and gloves on. Remember to pull your hood on."

"I got the deal for the pizza tonight. I hope that is okay. I mean we can order what you like when we get there."

"That will be great, is extra cheese, and pepperoni okay with you?" Val asked.

"That will be fine."

"Mommy, can I have a soda?"

"No, you can have milk or water."

"Rats."

"I better get my coat on, Val said.

"Here let me help you with that." James took her coat and held it for her. His hand brushed her shoulder as she put it on. Val's heart quickened a little. "I have to get some bags that are in the kitchen for the surprise tonight."

She went and picked up the bags, held them in one hand by the handles and walked back over to him.

James held his arm out for Val to take hold of. "Shall we?"

"All right then." They walked out the door and he closed the door behind them.

Fifteen minutes later they walked through the doors of the theater. The crowd had grown considerably since James picked up the tickets. Val looked around the room to see if Ben and Amy had arrived yet.

"Mommy look, they have cotton candy." Maggie pointed towards the concession stand. "Can I have some?"

"Maybe later. Now hand me your gloves, so you don't lose them."

Maggie drew a long breath as she took off her gloves and let out a sigh when she gave them to her mother.

Oh, the drama. Val smiled at the expression on her daughter's face.

"Where do we order the pizza?" James asked.

"Over at the concession stand and a waitress will bring the food and drinks to our seats." She noticed James giving her a puzzled look. "They remodeled the theater seats a few years ago. There are tables attached to each seat and they swing back and forth."

"Swing back and forth?" A questioning look crossed his face.

"You'll see."

"What would you like to drink?"

"Milk for Maggie, sweet iced tea for me."

"All right then."

"How about we meet you in line over by the board cutouts. Maggie and I get our picture taken every year?"

"Okay."

Val and Maggie headed towards the photo area. Val turned around for a moment and saw James standing in the pizza line. *He is a handsome man with a good soul.*

"Mommy, can we be the elves this time."

"Sure. Look over at the Santa and Mrs. Claus one."

"That's Ben and Amy." Maggie giggled.

"Sure is."

James walked up behind Val and placed his hand on the small of her back.

"Everything is ordered."

"Next." The photographer yelled.

"We'll be right back," Val said.

"Come on, Mommy."

They poked their heads through the cutouts. James also took several pictures of them. He laughed while Maggie made funny faces.

"Mommy, Mr. James can be the Grinch, I can be Max and you can be Cindy Lou Who."

"Are you game?" Val asked.

James hesitated for a moment. "The Grinch," he whispered.

"Sure."

He walked over to the stand and put his head through the board hole.

"Okay, everyone but the Grinch smile. Grinch you try to look sour."

Maggie and Val giggled.

After the photographer finished snapping the pictures, Val took James' hand.

"When do we get the pictures?" James asked.

"They will bring them to our seats, speaking of which we better get going, we don't want to miss the previews."

"All right."

"I forgot to tell you the waiters and waitresses are dressed in 1950's style Christmas outfits."

"Sounds festive," James said, a mocking tone in his voice.

"Okay Mr. Grinch. Where are our seats?"

"Row E seats 7, 8 and 9."

Once they reached their seats Maggie looked around the room and noticed Ben and Amy seated in the first row of the balcony.

"Mom, Amy and Ben are in the balcony."

"Oh, okay sit down. Our dinner will be here in a minute."

Val noticed the Bakers, the Robinsons, and Hal and Rose seated in the row in front of them. "I see the Robinsons made it this year."

"Yes, Rose had a special dinner for them last night. They were educating us about their latest geological discoveries somewhere in Brazil." James said.

"Last year they were in Spain on some sort of geological hunt. To tell the truth, I listened to a presentation they did at the church. I had no idea what they were talking about."

"I didn't have a clue last night either."

"Since it is Friday night, is your mother on a date with her neighbor friend?"

James looked at Val and she gave him the one eyebrow lifted expression.

"Inquiring minds want to know."

"They are going to dinner and to a concert."

"What concert?"

"Trans-Siberian Orchestra."

"So, your Mom rocks out."

"I didn't think so till now."

"Good for her."

"Pizza's here." James nodded at the waitresses approaching carrying their order.

Val smiled. "Okay I will let that conversation go."

"Thank you."

Val opened the armrest and pulled out the folding tray. Maggie and James did the same.

The two waitresses wore red 1950s style swing dresses with pearl necklaces. They both had their hair pulled back in a tight bun. Val smiled. *June Cleaver would be proud.*

"I've got one milk, two sweet teas and a medium extra cheese and pepperoni. Is that right?"

"Yes," James replied.

One waitress put plates, napkins and silverware on each foldout table and the other one handed out the drinks. "Would you like one slice of each?"

"Is that okay with you James? Val asked. "The crust is very thick."

"Sure."

The waitress opened the box and served the Sicilian style pizza.

"You didn't say it was Sicilian style."

"I wanted to see the surprised look on your face."

"These are huge slices."

Just then the lights went on and off.

"Five minutes warning before the movie starts. Maggie, do you like your pizza?"

"Yes, ma'am."

"What do you say?" Val whispered.

"Thank you, Mr. James."

"You're welcome."

"Thank you, Mr. James," Val whispered to him.

"You're welcome," he whispered.

Chapter Thirteen

Two hours later the lights came back on in the movie theater. Val and Maggie pushed their table aside and started to move. James hesitated for just a moment and then he did the same.

"Maggie, did you like the movie?"

"Yes ma'am, thank you Mr. James."

"You're welcome."

"Let's get your coat on" Val said.

"Me or Maggie?" James teased.

"Both, it was snowing when we came in remember?"

"That seems like a lifetime ago," James said.

"Are you knocking Christmas movies?"

"No, just musicals in general."

"Maggie, we have to do something about Ebenezer over here."

"Who is that?" Maggie asked.

"Scrooge."

"Oh, okay." Maggie looked at James. "You can't be a Scrooge; it is almost Christmas."

"I won't be."

"Promise?"

"Promise."

Val spied Mr. Jeffers as the trio walked into the lobby. She nodded her head toward the concession counter where he stood.

"We better get moving," she whispered to James. "We have a secret mission to complete."

"Okay," He kept his voice low. "What is this secret mission?"

"Spreading a little hope."

James gave Val a questioning look.

"You will see."

Ten minutes later, James parked his car in front of the Diner and the trio got out of the car.

"I am glad it stopped snowing." Val said.

"What are we doing at the diner?" James asked.

"We are not going to complete the mission here."

"Then where?"

"Over there," Val pointed at the spruce tree on Mr. Jeffers front lawn.

"Mr. Jeffers' place?"

"Yeah, if anyone needs some Christmas cheer it is that lonesome man. Now pop the trunk. We have a job to do."

"I don't know.

"Trust me."

Maggie tugged on Val's coat sleeve to get her to look down.

"What's up?"

"I made Mr. Jeffers a card can I put it by his door?"

"Let me see it."

Maggie pulled the card from her coat pocket and handed it to Val. The card had a yellow star on the front of it, and the inside read Merry Christmas from Santa's little elf.

"That is perfect. Hold my hand as we cross the street."

Side-by-side the three of them crossed the street.

"Okay, James and I will get started on the tree. You go put your card in the front door."

James pulled a box of Christmas lights from the bag and Val took out a silver Christmas star. Maggie started up the stairs, glanced back and pointed at Hal and Rose pulling their car into the parking space behind James' vehicle.

"What are you all up to?" Hal called as he closed the car door.

"Spreading a little Christmas hope," Val answered.

"Well, mind if we help?" Rose asked as she got out of the car.

Val looked over at Maggie as she walked back down the stairs.

"Well, what do you think Maggie? Can we let Mr. Hal and Mrs. Rose in our secret elf society?"

Maggie tapped her fingertip on her nose a few times.

"Hmm, I think so."

"Okay then let's get to work," Hal said. "I'll help you with those lights."

Rose pulled a box of red ornaments out of the bag.

"I got red and silver ornaments to match the wreath on the door," Val said.

Rose sighed as she looked at the ornaments. "I remember when this house was the most decorated one in town."

"Really?"

"Mrs. Jeffers was such a kind-hearted, beautiful woman and she dressed like Audrey Hepburn, always perfect. Mr. Jeffers used to make everyone laugh. This place looked like something out of a Christmas book every year. Wreaths on every window. White Christmas lights outlining the whole house. They had those huge light-up plastic Santa and Frosty figures on the porch. Right by this tree they had an actual sleigh. They threw a huge Christmas party every year. When I was just a teenager, I remember sitting on the stairs inside and watching Mr. and Mrs. Jeffers dance, it was like something out of a movie."

"What happened?" Val asked.

"They had a daughter. Her name was Emily." Rose looked over at Maggie for a moment. "She was a little older than Maggie when they discovered she had a rare form of leukemia. The wreath that is on the door used to hang in her hospital room, and I remember Mr. Jeffers put one of those plastic candles in the window. Sometimes my friends and I would just stop by and look at that candle and pray for Emily." Rose paused for a moment. "After she passed things were never the same. Mrs. Jeffers rarely left the house. No more parties. The only decoration she would put out was that wreath and a candle in the window. It was like time stopped for them."

"Wow. I never knew about any of this. What else can we do to help him?"

"I don't know. Maybe this will bring him around."

"We will think of something."

"Come on you two," Hal yelled. "We got a tree to finish. Where do I plug these lights in?"

"They are battery operated," James said.

"Oh."

"Maggie, would you like to put the star on top?"

"Yes, sir."

Val handed Maggie the star and James lifted her up. As Maggie put the star on Val smiled. My little girl is so grown up.

"Mommy."

"What honey?" Val snapped back to reality

"Is it straight?"

"It is perfect."

A few minutes later the group finished putting on the last of the ornaments and then stood back and admired their work. Val reached into the bag and pulled out a note and attached it to the tree with a clothespin.

"What is that?"

"A note that tells him how to turn the lights on and off."

"You think of everything," James said.

Maggie let out a huge yawn.

"I think that is our signal to head home," Val started. "We have a busy day tomorrow with all of the festivals and I know the diner will be busy. Rose, I will have the pie and cookies your ordered at the diner if you want to come by and pick them up?"

"Okay. Will you be able to come to dinner tomorrow night?" Rose asked.

"I apologize but I won't have time between the frosty festival and the give back festival."

"Next time then."

"Rose and Hal. Thank you for helping out."

"Our pleasure," Hal replied.

The group made their way back across the street to their vehicles.

"Goodnight," Val said.

"Goodnight, see you tomorrow," Rose answered.

Rose and Hal got in the car. Hal turned the ignition key and looked over at Rose. He saw the troubled look on her face.

"If those two really love each other then they will make it through the coming storm."

"I hope so because I can tell Val has really fallen hard for him."

James pulled into Val's driveway, braked to a stop and put the car in park. The snow had started back up again. He looked in the rearview mirror and saw Maggie sleeping.

"She is asleep," he whispered to Val.

"I am not surprised," Val whispered back. "Can you help me get her inside and I will make some coffee."

"Sure." They both quietly got out of the car. James opened the back door, unhooked Maggie's seatbelt and gathered Maggie in his arms. Val walked ahead and unlocked the front door. They went inside and Val carefully shut the door.

"Maggie's room is just down the hallway." Val headed down the hallway and opened the door. James carried Maggie into the room and put her on the bed. Val tiptoed over to Maggie and gently lifted her up and removed her coat. Then she laid her daughter down, moved over to Maggie's feet, and pulled off her boots. She saw James standing in the doorway, watching all of this. After pulling the blankets over Maggie's body, she bent over and kissed her on the forehead.

"Sweet dreams, my little one." Val walked towards the door.

"You are really good with her." He whispered as he stepped out into the hallway.

Val closed the door and turned toward him. "Thank you for saying that. Let's go to the living room. Would you like hot chocolate, coffee or maybe a glass of wine?" Val hoped she did not sound too nervous.

"Coffee would be great."

"Let me hang up your coat."

"Oh, Okay." He took off his coat and handed it to Val. She walked over to the coat rack and hung up both of their coats. "How good are you at building a fire?"

"You get the coffee going and I will get the fire started."

"Okay, Matches are in the silver box on the mantel." Val headed for the kitchen area. She pulled out a dark roast coffee pod for James and a French Vanilla one for herself.

"Do you use newspaper or fire starters?"

"Newspapers, you can use the ones on the coffee table."

James picked up the carefully folded papers. "Have you read these yet?"

"It's Christmas time, I don't have the minutes available. Besides, I already know most of what is going on in town."

"The benefits of owning a diner."

"Precisely."

James pulled a couple of logs out of the copper log holder and he put them on the fire grate. He rolled up a few sheets of newspaper and stuffed them in between the logs. Then he stood up and took the silver box off the mantel.

"This looks like an antique." He turned the box over, inspecting he design.

"Yes, it belonged to my husband's grandparents. One of the few things I kept from his side of the family after I sold our house in New York."

"I'm sorry I didn't mean to bring up the past."

"You could not have known. His grandparents were very nice to me. But they passed on before Maggie was born. Before you strike the match, did you open the chimney damper?"

"Um, let me double-check." James bent down and looked up the chimney. Then he opened the damper.

"Good thing I asked."

"Hey, I would have remembered."

"Before or after the smoke alarm went off?'

"Hopefully before."

Val gathered up the filled coffee mugs and walked towards James. He straightened up and took the cup she handed him. Val motioned him to toward the couch. After he sat down, she took a seat half a cushion away, facing him.

"This is a nice place."

"Thank you, I think of it as a work in progress."

"Meaning?"

"When I first got it, it was somewhat of a disaster. I had to have the kitchen and bathrooms remodeled, new plumbing, a new furnace put in, and then I remodeled Maggie's room."

"That was a lot of work."

"Still have mostly cosmetic work to do in this room, the guest room and my room. And if we stay, I plan on having a garage added on."

"If you stay? Do you have plans to move someplace else?"

"No, but you never know where life will lead." Val gazed into her coffee cup for a moment.

"So, what are the prices of admission for the Frosty Festivals and the Give Back one?"

"Nothing for the Give Back. Mostly the locals attend that one. The Frosty Festival is our Toys for Tots event, so one new toy per person.

"Oh."

"The toy store is a block from the movies. I am sure they will be open early tomorrow morning if you would like to get something."

"What did you buy?"

"Maggie will be donating a Baby Alive Doll and I am taking board games for the older kids. I got a chess set, Trouble, Connect Four, and Clue."

"Clue was one of my favorites."

"Mine too."

"What character did you pick?"

"Miss Scarlett, of course, and you?"

"Mr. Green."

"So, it was you who committed the murder in the conservatory with the candlestick?"

"No, that was Miss Scarlett in the ballroom with the wrench."

"Never."

"Never?"

"Miss Scarlett would have used the revolver, not a wrench."

"This conversation has taken a turn for the bizarre."

"Thank you for including Maggie this evening."

"It was my pleasure. She is a bright young girl."

"That she is."

"Thanks for helping out with the secret elf thing also."

"That was fun."

"I hope he will be pleasantly surprised."

"I think he will be," James said softly as he reached over and touched Val's arm. He leaned in for a kiss.

"Mommy!" Maggie yelled from her room.

Val jumped up almost spilling her coffee. "I think she must have had a nightmare. I will be right back."

Val slowly opened the door to Maggie's room and saw her sitting up in her bed and rubbing her eyes.

"Hey pumpkin what's wrong?" Val sat down on the bed next to Maggie and gently touched her face.

"I woke up and you weren't here."

"Did you have a bad dream?"

"Yes, there was a big snake."

"Where was the snake?'

"Under my bed."

"Under this bed?"

"Yes."

"I'll take care of that."

Val got up and then knelt on the floor. She lifted the bed skirt and looked under the bed.

"No snakes."

"Check the closet."

"Okay," Val got up and walked over to the closet and opened the door.

"Nope, no snakes."

Val noticed Maggie was still upset. She went back over to her bed and sat down.

"Come here little one." She opened her arms and Maggie crawled into her embrace.

"Would you like for me to sing to you like I used to?"

"Uh-huh."

"Lullaby and goodnight, with pink roses bedight, with lilies o'erspread, is my baby's sweet head." By the time Val got to the second verse Maggie was asleep again.

Val slipped out from the bed, tiptoed across the room, and headed back to the living room. James was stoking up the fire but turned when he heard Val enter.

"How is Maggie?"

"Oh, she is okay. Just a bad dream about giant snakes."

"Did I hear singing?"

"Yes, I hope I wasn't too bad."

"No, you weren't. It's just I haven't heard that song in a long time."

"Well, it's getting late and I have to get an early start tomorrow."

"Yeah, I better get going before the roads get too bad."

Side-by-side they walked over to the door. James grabbed his coat from the rack.

"Goodnight." He leaned over and kissed Val's check.

"Goodnight and thanks again for a fun evening."

James opened the door and walked out. Val watched from the bay window as he made his way to his car, then got in and backed out of her driveway.

James paced back and forth in his hotel room stopping every few minutes to re-read the article for his next story. He loaded the photos from the evening onto his computer. He had already read the same job threatening emails from his boss before starting to write his story.

"Get the story on Val or else. I really hate working for that jerk," James muttered.

He looked down at the clock on his laptop. Fifteen minutes left to meet the filing deadline. He read the story one more time, making sure it did not mention Val or Maggie. Just the facts about the movie festival and promises of coverage of the Frosty and Give Back Festivals. He smiled for a moment and added a line to the end of the story. Festive is a town full of magic and surprises during the Holiday Season.

"Shoot, I forgot to add the pictures." James clicked on the attachment icon and added the photo file. Then he shut his laptop and looked out the hotel window onto the quiet snow-covered landscape below.

Sunday is coming too fast. My day of reckoning for not telling Val the truth." He leaned against the wall for a moment and his shoulder sagged with the weight of his thoughts. Will she forgive me for not being completely honest? Will I lose her trust?

⮜Chapter Fourteen⮞

A t 7:00 a.m. the next morning, Val carried a sleeping Maggie in through the back door of the dinner. She nudged her office door open with her shoulder and sat her sleeping child on the couch. She tenderly removed Maggie's coat and boots. Then she turned Maggie and laid her down. Pulling the red blanket from the back of the couch, she gently covered her daughter.

Just then the door opened, and Amy peeked in.

"Val." She spoke in an excited tone.

"Quiet, Maggie is sleeping."

"I'm sorry," Amy whispered. "But you have got to come see this."

"What?"

"Come on."

Val put her purse down on her desk, and she hung her and Maggie's coats up on the rack. She walked into the dining area.

"Okay what is the big deal?" She spied Amy standing by the front door.

"Come look at the Jeffers' place."

Val walked over pretending like she didn't already know what the excitement was about. She looked out the window and caught a huge surprise herself. On the porch stood a large plastic Frosty the Snowman and Santa Claus.

"I have never seen that house so decorated," Amy said. "I wonder what got into him."

"Christmas."

"Well something sure did."

Val smiled. "We better get hopping; we should have a good crowd today. Chris and Thomas are coming in at nine to help out."

"Is Maggie staying here all day?"

"No, her friend Jeanie's Mom will pick her up at ten. They are going ice skating and then doing some Christmas shopping."

"Christmas shopping?"

"Yeah, apparently Briars Store has an area where kids can buy inexpensive gifts for their parents. One of the salesclerks helps them pick out the presents."

"That sounds like fun."

"Yeah, Maggie informed me this morning she wants to pick out my gift all by herself."

"She is growing up."

"Yeah, too fast. Okay, I will write the specials on the board and would you please get the coffee going?"

"I know what you mean about Christmas getting to people. Ben is treating his parents to lunch this afternoon; he hasn't done that the whole time we have been dating. Plus, last night after the festival he helped me decorate cookies."

Val finished writing the specials on the board and hung it back on the wall.

"Sometimes it takes a man a while to show that side of themselves to their significant other. The first Christmas Eve that Rich and I were together he tried to impress me by getting a huge live tree for my tiny apartment. He had no idea how to saw the bottom of the tree so it would fit into the stand, how many strands of lights were needed. His parents always hired professional decorators for their mansions. I remember that he went to three different stores to buy enough fairy lights and he made a star out of tin foil for the top of the tree. That was a great Christmas."

"Did you get engaged then?"

"No, we got engaged the following January 21st. That was his birthday. We were walking in Central Park by the Angel of the Waters Statute. He knew I loved that area of the park. He got down on one knee and said the greatest gift he could ever receive would be my marrying him."

"Did you have a huge wedding?"

"No, his parents didn't think that I was right for their son. Plus, we didn't want the press there. So, we had a small church wedding and a reception at the Calvert Historic Inn in Annapolis. His parents did show up, but they were acting like snobs the whole time. Promptly left right at the end of the reception for a trip to Paris."

"Pardon my asking but why did your husband work for them?"

"I think he hoped they would change. When he realized that wouldn't happen, he wanted to leave but ...." Val turned her head away from Amy, so she would not see the tears.

"Hey, let's get some Christmas music going. How about John Mellencamp's *I Saw Mommy Kissing Santa Claus.*" Amy suggested.

"Yeah, that will work."

"Will Maggie wake up?"

"That's okay, I have to get her up in a few minutes anyway. She wouldn't want to miss out on Mr. Jeffers coming in for breakfast."

"They are becoming great friends. Sort of like the Grandfather and Granddaughter thing."

"You just gave me an idea." Val headed for the kitchen door.

"Is that a good thing?"

"Very."

Val opened the door to her office and found Maggie sitting up on the couch putting on her shoes.

"I was about to wake you up." She walked into the room and sat down on the couch next to her daughter.

"I can't wait to go ice skating today."

"Don't forget I put the toy for the Frosty Festival in your backpack. Along with your ice skates and an extra pair of gloves."

"I wish you could go with me."

"I know honey, I wish I could too, but I have to work. Now I have something special to show you this morning."

"Really, what is it?"

"Come on let's go look at Mr. Jeffers's house."

They walked into the dining area together and once they reached the front door, Val said, "Look across the street at his front porch."

"Santa and Frosty," Maggie yelled.

"See what a little Christmas spirit can do," Val whispered.

Just then they noticed Mr. Jeffers open his front door.

"Now I have an idea."

"What?"

Val bent down and whispered something into Maggie's ear.

"Is that okay?"

"Yes ma'am."

"Good, now go sit at the counter and I'll get your breakfast started."

Maggie skipped back towards the counter as Val watched Mr. Jeffers cross the street. She opened the door as he approached the entryway.

"Good Morning, Mr. Jeffers."

"Good Morning, Val." He said

"Let me hang your coat for you."

He took his coat and hat off and handed it to Val. Then he gave a thank you nod.

"Amy has the coffee going." Val motioned toward the counter.

"I'll have the buttermilk pancakes this morning with a side of bacon." He said as he walked to the counter and sat down next to Maggie.

"Amy, would you get a glass of milk for Maggie please?"

"Sure."

"Good Morning, Maggie, Amy."

"Good Morning, Mr. Jeffers," Maggie answered. "I like your Santa and Frosty."

"Thank you."

Amy placed a full mug of coffee on the counter in front of Mr. Jeffers and a glass of milk for Maggie."

"Mr. Jeffers would you like regular cream or maybe the peppermint creamer?"

"Regular. Oh, Amy, would Ben be available later today? Seems that the light for my Frosty the Snowman is not working and I think the cord needs to be replaced."

"He will be here in a few minutes, so I can ask him."

"Thank you."

"I am going ice skating today." Maggie announced.

"That sounds like fun." Mr. Jeffers said.

"Can you come?"

Mr. Jeffers laughed. "Maggie, I am afraid with these old bones I don't skate anymore."

"Rats," she sighed. "We are going to put up our Christmas tree tomorrow."

"That sounds like fun too."

Val walked into the room carrying both of their breakfast plates.

"Mr. Jeffers, one pancake special with sausage and for you; Maggie one pancake special with a bowl of strawberries."

"Thank you, Mama."

"You're welcome."

Val walked over to the cash register and straightened up the menus and she glanced over at Maggie. Maggie looked at her and Val gave her an encouraging wink.

"Mr. Jeffers," she started. "Mommy and I would like for you to come to our house for Christmas dinner."

Val walked back and faced them. "We would love it if you would come."

Mr. Jeffers looked down at his food for a moment.

"Thank you, it would be an honor."

"The honor is ours, and dinner will be at three o'clock."

Just then the front door opened, and seven customers crowded in.

"Here we go, Amy." Val went over to the group "Merry Christmas everyone. Are you all together?"

"Just the three of us." One man answered as he pointed at two other people. Val guessed was his family, since they wore Christmas sweaters that matched.

"Sit in whatever booths you would like. Amy will be over for your order in just a moment. And if you are so inclined the jukebox is free today. Breakfast specials are listed on the chalkboard."

At 9:00 a.m. James walked into the crowded dinner. The only empty seat that was open was located at the counter.

He quickly looked around the room, searching for Val. But she was nowhere in sight. He noticed Ben and Mr. Jeffers were talking and Rose was sitting at one of the tables with the Bakers.

"James, come over here and join us." Rose signaled to him.

He worked his way toward their booth. "Good Morning everyone. Boy, it sure is busy in here this morning. I had to circle the block four times before a parking space opened up."

Rose moved over so he could sit down. "This is the busiest day of the festivals."

"Why did they schedule two festivals for one day?" Mrs. Baker asked. "I don't remember it being that way before."

"The company that owns the outdoor ice rink was only available for this weekend, and we are getting close to the end."

"We still have the baking contest next week?" Mrs. Baker added.

"That is Hal's favorite."

Just then Val walked through the door carrying several orders. She stopped at the booth next to theirs, glanced over and smiled at James. He swallowed hard as he watched her pass out the food to the customers. She walked over to their table.

"So, what can I get for you today? Wait a minute where is Hal?"

"At the bank getting a check. We decided to buy the house next to the Inn. Ben assured us that he can do most of the work to fix it up to our standards and we want our kids to have their own space when they come to visit."

"That is great news."

"I have more great news for you, Cal and Shelvey had to cancel their reservation."

"Since when is a cancellation good news?" James asked.

"I think that means they are brand new grandparents," Val added.

"Benjamin and Bryan made their debut at 5:28 and at 5:34 this morning."

"Well, tell them I said congratulations."

"I am sure they will text me several pictures before the day is over."

"Who is catering tonight's event?"

"The pub is handling the main dishes and the Tea Room has the desserts and drinks."

"Thank goodness it is not me this year. Come 5:00 p.m. I am off for the weekend. Much needed R and R," Val smiled.

"Val," James looked down at the tabletop for a moment. "Tomorrow, I was wondering if we could go to the tea-room for a little while."

"Maggie has play practice after church and I do have to get a Christmas tree. So how about we meet there while Maggie is at rehearsal. They open at noon."

"Okay."

"So, what can I get everyone this morning?"

As soon as Val entered the kitchen Chris and Thomas walked through the back door.

"I am so glad you are here," Val said.

"I had to park by the Chamber of Commerce," Chris shrugged out of his coat and hung it up.

"Well, no time to waste guys. Table seven, four and six need to be cleaned and table one needs their orders taken."

"When does the rest of the crew get here?"

"At ten."

"All right, Thomas, let's hit it."

At that moment the phone rang, and Val walked over to the wall and took the receiver off the phone. "Memories Diner.... Okay thanks. I will get her out there... Amy."

Amy hurried into the kitchen.

"Orders up table three and I have to get Maggie ready. Ask Chris to take care of these orders for Rose's table please."

"Got it."

Val almost ran to her office and grabbed Maggie's coat, backpack and boots and headed for the dining area. "Come on little one, Jeanie's Mom is outside, and we got to run. Here get your boots on."

"Okay," Maggie quickly got her boots on.

Val handed her daughter her coat and Maggie put it on.

"The toy and your skates are in your backpack."

"Yes, ma'am."

"Let's go." Val motioned here toward the door.

"Goodbye, Mr. Jeffers."

"Goodbye, Maggie."

Val and Maggie headed for the door.

"Val really needs some help with Maggie," Mrs. Baker said.

"Don't let her hear you say that. She is so exhausted that she doesn't even realize it." Rose answered.

James looked down at the table. "So, when will you settle on the new house?"

"Monday. Ben is going to do most of the work on it. We just need to hire an electrician for some of the upgrades."

"What needs renovation?" Mr. Baker asked.

"The bathrooms need to be redone and we decided to replace the carpet in the living room with hardwood floors. Paint the kitchen cabinets, new tile for the kitchen floor and replace the appliances. Paint the outside to match the inn and paint the interior. Oh, I almost forgot, replace the windows in the living room and dining area."

"Seeing as how hard Ben works, that won't take him long." Mr. Baker said.

"I know a little secret that may pre-occupy him for a while." Rose grinned at everyone.

"Now what are you up to?" James asked.

"Just you wait and see."

Val rushed back inside and headed straight for the kitchen, almost crashing into Chris as he came out the door. He suddenly stopped, balancing the orders on his tray.

Ben got up from his seat and shook Mr. Jeffers's hand.

"I will drop by tomorrow around two o'clock to take a look at that Frosty for you," he said.

"Thank you, young man." Mr. Jeffers replied.

Ben stopped by Rose's table on his way towards the door.

"Good morning everyone."

"Good morning," they replied in chorus.

"Ben, everything you need for your special surprise is in our kitchen. Hal should be back at the Inn by now." Rose said.

"Thank you, ma'am. I am heading over to the candy store now to get some extra gifts."

"That is a good idea young man."

Rose saw Amy walk out of the kitchen.

"You better get moving, before Amy makes her way over here," Rose whispered.

"All right then." He walked over toward the counter area. Tapped Amy's shoulder, and gave her a kiss on the cheek.

"I will pick you up this afternoon."

"We are closing today at five o'clock," Amy said.

"Got it." He headed for the door.

"Mr. Jeffers would you like another cup of coffee?"

"No, Thank you. I have a question for you."

"Yes, sir."

"In my day people took gifts for the hostess when they are invited to a special dinner. Do people still do that?"

"Sometimes."

"What should I take Val?"

"She likes tea, so maybe something from the Tea Room. I know she does like the lemon white chocolate truffles that you can get at the candy store."

"Thank you."

"You're welcome. How much do I owe you today?"

"Seven dollars and fifty cents."

Mr. Jeffers pulled a twenty out of his pocket and handed it to her.

"Let me get your change."

"No, you keep it today."

"Are you sure?"

"Yes, Merry Christmas."

"Merry Christmas. Mr. Jeffers."

He got up and headed for the front door. While he was putting on his coat, the door opened, and four more customers entered. They shuffled their feet on the large welcoming mat, laughing amongst themselves.

"Back to the grindstone," Amy said and glanced at the group letting out her own contagious chuckle. "They really seem to be enjoying this weather."

"Too many tourists." Mr. Jeffers grumbled.

Later that afternoon James wandered around the Frosty Festival, half-heartedly taking pictures of people ice-skating, the vendor displays and of course Frosty and Santa Claus. He interviewed a few of the craft vendors about their items and how the festival brought in revenue for the town. He wandered into the food tent and surveyed the room. The gyro vendor that was at the Lights On Festival was there along with several others. After a few moments standing in line, he felt a tap on his shoulder. He turned around and saw Hal standing there.

"Good afternoon, are you enjoying the festival?"

"Yes." James shrugged.

"Got Val on your mind."

"Yeah and Maggie."

"I am going to go over get some fried chicken, so why don't you sit with me once you get your food."

"Okay."

"You may want to get some hot cider from the Davis Farm Stand, theirs is the best."

"All right."

"What would you like, sir?" The vendor asked.

"One chicken gyro and chips."

"That will be $5.50." The man gave him a sturdy paper plate filled with his food.

"Thank you." James reached into his wallet and gave the guy a ten. "Keep the change."

After getting a cup of cider, James turned and searched the tent area. He noticed Hal at one of the tables on the far side of the tent. He slowly made his way over. He saw a small table next to theirs with a reserved sign on it. There was a rose-filled vase, candles and what appeared to be a cake box on it.

"What is that all about?" James asked as he nodded toward the table. He carefully sat down trying not to spill his cider.

"Oh, probably someone popping the question. That happens a few times during the festivals. I heard a young couple from North Carolina got engaged at the Lights on Festival. Another couple got engaged at the Movie Festival."

"Tis the season."

"That fried chicken looks good."

"They make it with Old Bay seasoning." Hal took a bite, chewed and swallowed, then lifted his eyebrows and looked at James then spoke again.

"You look like you lost your best friend."

"Tomorrow is the day, I tell Val."

"Nervous?"

"Yeah."

"Have you spoken to your mother yet about your job situation?"

"Not really."

"Humph."

"What does the humph mean?" James stared at Hal.

"You need to ask yourself what you really want and what you are willing to fight for."

"It is not so easy."

"Maybe it's easier than you think."

"What do you mean?"

"I know that you care about Val and Maggie. That is evident to anyone who sees you all together. Are you willing to take a chance on that? As far as your mother goes, parents are sometimes ready to move forward and those of us closest to them are the last to notice or realize it, or don't want to realize what is going on. It was that way for me when my father passed on. My mother lived with us for a few months while her house was on the market for sale. I wanted her to stay longer with me and Rosie. Mother insisted that she get her own apartment and she was happy there. She liked having her independence back. Maybe your mother is ready to move on with her life."

"I don't know about that."

"You don't know until you ask."

"What about Val? Any advice for that situation?"

"If you love her stick around and don't give up."

A little while later Val and Maggie walked into the food tent. She surveyed the room looking for an empty seat when she spotted the reserved table. A smiled spread over her face.

"Mommy can I get a crab sandwich?'

"Yes, you can have a crab cake sandwich and some chips."

They walked toward the seafood stand and got in line.

"Did you have a good time today with Jeanie and her Mom?"

"Yes ma'am. We skated and I only fell two times."

"Did you hurt yourself?"

"No, I fell on my butt."

"Next," a gruff voice yelled.

Val turned and had to look down to see the very short almost bald man in front her, wearing a gray tee-shirt, jeans and a torn white apron that hung past his knees.

"Two crab-cake sandwich combos with lettuce and mayo, on soft rolls with chips, a sweet tea for me and a milk for her."

"That'll be $17.50," he growled back, as he arranged their food on two throw-away dishes. He filled two cups with their drinks, put it all on a tray and reached up to give it to her.

Val handed him the money and took the food.

"Let's go sit over by that table near the roses," she told Maggie.

"Okay."

As they headed for the table Val noticed Amy and Ben at the hot cider stand.

Maggie looked at her daughter as they sat down.

"Mommy, why are you smiling funny?"

"Love is in the air."

"Huh?"

"You will understand when you're older … say around thirty." Val handed Maggie her food.

"So, what about your shopping trip?"

"They had one room that had all sorts of stuff in it and a lady that was dressed like an elf showed me different things I could buy."

"Are you sure she wasn't a real elf?"

"No, she was too big."

"Did you buy something?"

"Yes ma'am."

"Well don't tell me, I want to be surprised."

Val watched for a moment as Ben and Amy made their way to the reserved table and she heard Amy giggle. So far so good.

"After we finish here, we will go see Santa. What are you going to ask him for?" *Please don't say a puppy*

"A castle for my Disney dolls, a pasta maker and a car for my dolls."

"A pasta maker like I have?"

"No, like Jeanie has."

Note to self, ask Jeanie's Mom about that one.

"What are you going to ask Santa to bring for Mommy?"

Before Maggie could answer, they heard Amy yell "Yes!"

Val turned and saw Ben getting up off his knees and Amy hugging him. The whole crowd started to applaud.

"What happened Mommy? Why is Ms. Amy jumping up and down?"

"She is very happy."

"Why?"

"Because she is going to get married."

"Today?"

"Not today. Now hurry up and finish your sandwich. After we see Santa, we will get dessert at the Giveback Festival. Okay?"

"Okay."

Val glanced over at the effervescent Amy. *Can I be that happy again?*

Chapter Fifteen

Forty-five minutes later Val and Maggie walked into the main lobby of the Chamber of Commerce. The building at one time was the library and the large two-story lobby still had an elegant style. Through the crowd, she saw standing in front of the large stained-glass window was an eleven-foot-tall Christmas tree decorated with white lights and antique Victorian style crystal Christmas ornaments. Several leather-sofas lined the walls. There was a grand, wooden staircase that led to the second-floor offices with green garland and red ribbon braided around the banisters. The wooden floor inlay pattern reminded Val of some of the older homes she had seen in the homes of New York.

"Val, over here," She heard Rose call out, and she turned to her left and saw Rose standing behind what was once the library checkout counter. Next to that was a smaller Christmas tree with name tags on it. On the other side of the stand sat the orchestra members tuning up their instruments. Wait staff traveled through the crowd with their trays of drinks, desserts and hors d'oeuvres.

"Come on, let's say hi to Mrs. Rose." Val took Maggie's hand while they made their way through the crowd.

"Good evening Rose. Where is Hal?"

"Oh, he's upstairs showing James some of the interesting architectural points of this building."

Val's heart jumped a little when Rose mentioned James' name.

"Is Chris here yet?" Val asked.

"I saw him a few minutes ago. It is hard to keep track of people with this crowd. The Bakers are here somewhere. You have got to try the cherry cheesecake desserts."

"Can I have one Mom?"

"I will get one in a minute."

"I guess you heard the big news."

"I saw it happen. I hope people keep things off Facebook until they have a chance to tell their parents."

"Amy's parents already knew. Ben did the old-fashioned thing and asked for her hand and Amy's father helped him pick out the engagement ring."

"That is sweet." Val felt a pang of sadness. "How many names on the tree?"

"One hundred and sixty-four. We will keep filling it up as people choose names."

"So, who is giving the opening speech this year?"

"Yours truly."

"Mom, can I get a piece of chocolate cake?"

"I'll be back in a minute," Val told Rose.

Val and Maggie headed toward one of the waiters and tapped him on the shoulder.

"What would you like?" he asked.

"You only get one choice for dessert." Val said.

"Cheesecake, please."

He handed Maggie the plate of dessert along with a fork.

"Thank you."

"What will you have?"

"Nothing for me tonight. Thank you for asking." Val surveyed the room for a couple of places for them to sit down.

"There are a couple of spaces by the big Christmas tree. Let's head over that way. Be careful with your cake."

"Yes ma'am."

James walked with Hal down the main staircase, when he noticed Maggie and Val sitting on one of the couches by the large tree. One part of him wanted to hide somewhere in the building, but the other part was drawn to them. He decided to listen to that side of his brain that took him their way.

"Good evening," he spoke and approached them.

"Hello, where's Hal? Rose said he was with you."

"He is helping Rose get started. Hi Maggie, do you like the cheesecake?"

"Yes, sir. It is yummy. I had a crab cake for dinner, that was yummy too. Mommy took me to see Santa."

"She did? What did you ask Santa for?"

"A castle, I wanted to ask him for a puppy, but I forgot."

Val's eyes went wide when the word puppy was mentioned ... again.

Just then the orchestra drummer played a little fanfare to get everyone's attention.

"Saved by the bell ...drum ...sort of," Val smiled at James.

Rose stood in front of the Christmas giving tree.

"Good evening everyone. I want to thank you all for turning out this year to help members of our community. It is no secret that this is my favorite festival. Here we get to show the world what our town of Festive is about and that is caring for each other in good times and rough ones. I want to take a moment to thank this year's committee for putting everything together. This year there are one hundred and sixty-four names to choose from. So please mull around and stop by and pick a name or two. Enjoy the music, the food, and the company. Don't forget to stop by the stand here and let one of the committee members know what name you have chosen so we can keep track of things. That's all folks." She walked over to the tree and pulled off one of the tickets. The orchestra started playing *O Holy Night.*

"Shall we go choose a name, Maggie Sue?"

"Okay."

"James, you are welcome to stand in line with us if you would like."

"Sure." James turned and lifted his camera to his face. "I just want to get a few pictures of this first."

Once they were at the tree Val looked at Maggie. "Do you want to choose, or should I pick one."

"You pick one."

"Okay." Val looked at a few cards and pulled one from the tree.

"Mr. James, are you getting a ticket?"

James cleared his throat and he looked at Maggie's big smile for a moment. Then he walked over to the tree, read a few cards and pulled one from the tree.

Val smiled as they walked over to Rose.

"Whose ticket did you have?"

"Carrie's Dad."

"Hal and I chose her boys."

"Is her Dad home from the hospital yet?"

"They hope he will be home for Christmas."

"James, whose name did you pick?"

"The Dixons."

"Well, I hope you know how to use a hammer and swing an axe," Hal said as he walked up behind him. "Ben just called me, he asked me to pick a name for him and Amy. Seems they are a little preoccupied this evening."

"I will pick it." Rose volunteered. She pulled a tag off the tree and handed it to Val.

"Pearl Johnson. Amy will love this."

"Why?" James asked.

"Pearl Johnson was her first-grade teacher, and Amy adores her."

Just then Maggie let out an over the-top-yawn.

"I think that is my sign to get this one home. We have a lot to do tomorrow. Goodnight, everyone."

"Goodnight, see you at church tomorrow," Rose said.

"Let me walk you out," James volunteered.

"That's okay we got a close parking space, so stay and enjoy the music."

"I will see you tomorrow at the tearoom then?'

"Yeah, at noon."

Maggie yawned again.

"Come on Maggie Sue, let's go before you turn into a pumpkin."

"How do I do that?" Maggie asked.

"That is just an expression."

James watched mother and daughter walk out the lobby door and he continued to stare as the doors closed behind them. Someone bumped into him and brought him back to reality. He turned back toward the giving tree and saw the Bakers heading toward him.

"I understand you chose a ticket this year." Mrs. Baker said.

"Yes, I did. I have the Dixons." James replied.

"Oh, they live near Val. The white house on the corner with the green shutters. They were at Val's Christmas dinner last year." Mr. Baker said. "We picked the Brooks family this year. They have several foster kids staying with them."

"I think Chris picked the Boys and Girls Club. They need help with putting up new basketball stands, and I overheard Rose say Ben got Victoria's house," Mrs. Baker added.

"Who is Victoria?" James asked.

"Victoria's house is a place people can stay for free while their loved one is in the hospital. The town set that up since there are so many tourists that come here, and in case something happens. That way people don't have to worry about an added hotel bill on top of a hospital bill. They give a Christmas party for the families."

"That's nice."

"Yeah, well that is what this town is all about and why we love to visit."

Twenty minutes later James was pacing in his room. He picked up his phone, and then tossed it back down on his bed. He walked into the bathroom, bent over the sink and rinsed his face. Grabbing the towel off the rack, dried his face and then tossed it to the floor. He peered at the phone again from the bathroom doorway. Then he walked over to the bed, picked up his phone and punched in his mother's number.

"Hello James, I just got home. Harvey and I went out to dinner. You have got to try the new Italian restaurant next to my hairdresser. I can't remember the name right now."

"Ma, I have to talk to you' James quietly said.

"Oh my … I have got to sit down. Are you all right? Are you sick?'

"No, Ma, I'm in love."

"Give me a heart attack. Why didn't you say so? Have some mercy on your old mother."

"But I think I blew it."

"Okay, start from the beginning."

"You watch the cooking channels; do you remember the chef Val Young?"

"Yeah, I think so. Didn't something happen with her husband and her baby? I seem to remember reading something about that years ago."

"Yeah, her husband died in a car accident and his parents tried to get custody of her daughter."

"I remember now their pictures were all over the gossip pages."

"Well she owns a small diner here in Festive and ..."

"She is the one you are in love with."

"Yes, but."

"What did you do?"

"Because of what happened to her in New York gossip columns and paparazzi following everywhere she went, Val hates reporters."

"Oh ...Oh no, don't tell me James Edward Hawk that you have not told her the truth."

"No, I didn't know about everything until I found out that she hated reporters, and then I kept quiet."

"A lie by omission is still a lie, I taught you that James."

"I know and I am telling her the truth tomorrow."

"Good."

"But there is another thing."

"More problems."

"I may need to stay here to fix things."

"For how long?"

"I don't know."

"Do you think she loves you?"

"Yes, I think so and I love her little girl Maggie too. Ma Val is an amazing woman."

"What about your job?'

"I hate working for Bryon. The man is a dictator. So, I am thinking about quitting. But I'm worried about you and helping out with the bills."

"Glory be to Saint Agnes. James, you are my son and I love you, but you are so dense sometimes. You must get that from your father."

"What do you mean?"

"I have been wanting to sell the house for the last six months, why do you think I have been reading all of those brochures about retirement communities for."

"I thought they just came in the mail."

"Harvey and I have been wanting to move to one of those places where everything is included. A small apartment, dining halls. We even saw a place that has a bank, beauty salon, pub, library, travel club, and college classes. I have been waiting on you to move out."

"You and Harvey?"

"We have been dating for months now. We don't just play canasta all the time."

"Ma, too much information."

"Oh, my son, you have a lot to learn about life."

"Okay, Ma,"

"So, what about Christmas?"

"I don't know about that yet. I guess it depends on what happens tomorrow."

"Be gentle when you tell her and be patient. I know you can be patient... you get that from me."

"Okay, I will try."

"That's my son. Call me tomorrow once you have talked to her."

"I will."

"Goodnight."

"Goodnight, Ma."

"I must be so dense," he whispered as he shut off his phone. "My mother and Harvey. That is way too much information."

Val and Maggie arrived just a few moments before the service started. They hurried to their usual spot at the fourth pew from the front of the church. As she started to sit down Val could feel that someone was staring at her back. She glanced around the sanctuary and noticed Wallace Simpson glaring at it.

I wonder what that is all about.

A little while later after receiving communion and she was returning to her seat, she felt that same stare boring into her.

Okay, that is freaking me out.

James carried the bagel he bought from the local bakery up to his room. He grabbed his phone from the side table and noticed several voice messages from his mother. He punched in his code.

"Son, you are confusing your mother. If you hadn't told Val yet about your job, why did you include pictures of her with your article? You're playing with fire there my boy."

"What is she talking about?" James pulled up the link to the newspaper on his phone and scrolled through the site.

"No, no, no." he slammed the phone on his bed.

He snatched up the phone again and read the article.

"Bryon... that jerk!" He grabbed his keys and coat and headed for the door.

After the end of the service, Val put her coat on. She bent down and hugged Maggie.

"Okay pumpkin, I have an errand to run. After rehearsal is over, I'll pick you up here and we can get our Christmas tree."

"Okay, Mom."

Val headed for the back of the church and Wallace followed her. Val turned and faced him.

"Wallace, is something going on? You have been glaring at me all through the service."

"I'll say something is wrong, I have followed your rules about no last names and no pictures of you or Maggie in the paper. But you let someone else write about you and put pictures of you and Maggie at the film festival in the Chicago paper. My cousin sent me the link this morning."

Val started shaking and she grabbed the pew. "What are you talking about?"

Wallace pulled his phone out of his jacket and handed it to her. Val scrolled through the article.

"What is this? Who? Former celebrity chef, widow of Rich Young and her daughter spend the night attending the Festive Film Festival. Oh..." She read aloud. She took a deep breath and read the rest of the article to herself. Val Young is the owner of the Memories diner. Years ago, after her husband's death, she had to fight for custody of her daughter and then she vanished from the New York scene. Tears ran over her cheeks. "Who wrote this? Has this gone viral?"

"Yes, Read the by-line."

"James Hawk. I am going to be sick. I have to get out of here before Maggie sees me."

"You didn't know?"

"No, of course not."

"Val, I am sorry." He reached his hand out to her.

"I've got to get myself together and think. I was supposed to meet James at the tearoom." She grabbed her phone and texted James.

"Meet me at the diner."

"Are you okay to drive?"

"No, I will walk there."

"No, I will drive you there."

This hurts so bad. Val turned her head away from him for a moment. "Let's go."

Val sat in one of the diner booths her gaze locked on the glass of water Wallace had gotten for her. He had offered to stay but she told him to leave. She looked around the room for a moment and saw the mistletoe hanging over the jukebox. *I almost kissed him. What about Maggie what if one of her friends sees this? What a smooth liar he is.*

A key tap on the door brought her back to reality. She looked up and saw James standing there. *Fraud.* She walked over to the door twisted the deadbolt open and turned away from him as he swung it open and walked in, then closed it behind him.

"I guess you read the article."

"Yeah, Wallace showed me. I wasn't about to have this conversation in public. I will say this for you, you are one smooth operator. Tell me something," she turned and faced him. "Were you just playing me this whole time for a story? Or what? Did you even consider how my daughter can be hurt by all of this? Me, or are we just another by-line to you. I mean I thought the reporters in New York were bad, but you are a snake in the grass."

"Val, let me explain please," He moved toward her, and she took a step back.

"Explain what?" she yelled.

"I sent those pictures by mistake. I was tired and rushing to get my story done and I attached the wrong folder to the email. Plus, I didn't write those things about you. My boss did. Ever since I found out who you are, he has been hounding me to get a story on you and I refused to write it, so he added that whole paragraph."

"Oh, so that makes everything okay." She mocked back. "This is just some sort of mistake. You lied to me this whole time. I told you how I feel about reporters. What they did to me and Maggie. You didn't say one word. Are there other stories out there that I don't know about?"

"No,"

"Why should I believe you?"

"I didn't write any other story about you. I can show you what I have written. I am so sorry; I didn't tell you. That is why I wanted to meet with you today, so I could come clean about my job."

"You should have told me from the beginning"

"I should have yes, there is no excuse for how I acted, but then, I fell in love with you."

"You what?"

"I fell in love with you and Maggie."

"You fell in love with me, really. I don't believe you. Who else knows you are a reporter?"

"Hal, Rose, Ben and the Mayor, but they thought I had told you already. When I told Hal that I hadn't he told me that I needed to do this right away before you found out the hard way."

"To think what a fool I have been. I allowed myself to think, to dream again, even. I had you over to my house. I let you near my child. "

"Val, I am so sorry. I don't know how to fix this. Please let me try." He walked towards her again arms out, with his hands palms up in a pleading gesture.

"Try to fix this, get out. Get out of my diner now. I don't want to see you; I don't want you near Maggie ever again. Get out now."

He turned with his shoulder slumped and headed for the door. He turned and looked at Val again.

"I know you don't believe me, but I never meant to hurt you and I do love you."

Val's angry tears stung her eyes as she looked at him.

"Leave."

He turned back toward the door and walked out. She walked over and locked the door behind him.

Val looked at the clock over the jukebox. Time to go back for her daughter.

"I have got to get myself together." She slowly gathered up her purse and walked down the hallway to the restroom. She looked in the mirror at her tear-stained face. "I have been such a fool." She washed her face and pulled Visine out of her purse. Put a few drops in her eyes. Pull it together you have got to stay strong for Maggie.

Chapter Sixteen

James slowly walked into the lobby of the Inn. He noticed Hal and Rose standing next to the fireplace. Rose had a silver tray in her hands. He tried to continue quietly toward the stairs.

"James," Hal called out. "We were just talking about you."

James paused turned toward them, and Rose let out a soft gasp.

"From the look on your face I gather things did not go well." Rose spoke as she placed the cookie tray on the coffee table.

James took off his coat and slumped down into one of the chairs.

"Val found out before I could tell her."

"How?" Hal asked.

"I attached the wrong file to an email I sent to my boss, he added pictures of her and Maggie to the last article I wrote. Plus, he added information about Val's past. The death of her husband, the custody battle. I tried to explain to her that I didn't write that, but she didn't believe me, and she thinks I played her for a story. She is scared about how this may hurt Maggie. I told her that I loved her and that I was sorry, but she threw me out of the diner and said she doesn't want to see me and doesn't want me around Maggie."

"Oh, no," Rose sighed. "I was afraid something like this would happen."

"She may be mad at you also, she asked me if anyone else knew and I told her the truth. I also told her that you were the ones who told me to tell her."

"Don't worry about that. Val needs to cool off a bit and calm down." Hal started. "This must have been a shock, right down to her core."

"Where is she now?" Rose asked.

"She had mentioned something before about getting a Christmas tree today, so she and Maggie can decorate it."

"Well that will give her something else to concentrate on for a little while," Rose added.

"What should I do now? Should I try to call her? Text her?"

"No, give her a day to try and calm down."

"I have a call to make." James got up. "I will see you later I guess." He headed for the stairs.

"I better call Val and apologize." Rose said.

"Call her later tonight. Let her have this afternoon with Maggie and give her a chance to settle," Hal advised.

"Okay."

Maggie sat quietly in the back seat of the van. Val looked into her rear-view mirror and saw her staring at her feet.

"Did everything go okay at play rehearsal?" Val asked.

"Yes, ma'am."

"Do you like our Christmas tree?"

"Yes, ma'am."

"Why are you so quiet?"

"I kept forgetting my lines during practice, and the director got mad I said waddling clothes instead of swaddling clothes"

"I can help you with that."

"Okay."

"Feel better?"

"Yes ma'am…. Mommy why are you sad."

"Mommy got some bad news today about someone she knew."

"Are they sick?"

"Sort of. But you know what, we are almost home. We have a gigantic Christmas tree to put up and I happen to have everything we need to make my double stuffed sugar cookies."

"With sprinkles?"

"With extra sprinkles."

"Yay," Maggie laughed.

James sat down on his bed, turned on his laptop computer, and opened his email. Scrolling down the list he opened the one from Bryon.

"Great article about the film festival, thanks for including the pictures of Val Young and her daughter. I took the liberty of adding their information to the story. Still looking for that full-story on her though."

"Jerk!!! Thanks for messing up my life." James closed his laptop and his phone rang.

James looked at the caller ID and sighed.

"Hello, Mom."

"I have been worried about you all morning, tell me what happened."

"Val is furious, and she doesn't want to see me again."

"Why did you add the pictures of them to the article?"

"I didn't mean too. I attached the wrong file to the email and Bryon edited the story to match the photos."

"He is a snake."

"I agree, but I am the one that really messed up."

"Do you love her?"

"Yes."

"Does she love you?"

"She said something about starting to have feelings for me."

"That is code for she was starting to fall in love with you."

"But I blew it."

"Maybe things can be salvaged."

"Ma, she threw me out of her diner."

"She is just angry, maybe once she has a chance to calm down …."

"I don't think so, Mom. She is scared that Maggie can be hurt by this."

"How are you going to fix things?"

"I don't know." James waited for his mother to answer. "Ma, are you still there?"

"Yes, I'm coming to Festive."

"No, Mom."

"Don't no Mom me. I am coming to Festive and we will fix this."

"Mom the costs."

"Harvey used to work for the airlines, he gets discounts all the time. I will get him to book us the tickets."

"Mom!"

"James Edward Hawk don't argue with me. I'm your mother, and we will fix this. I will send you my itinerary. Now get us a room at the hotel."

"Yes, ma'am."

"All right then, give me a few minutes to call Harvey."

"Okay, Mom." He hung up.

"Just what I need, my mother and her boyfriend here." He muttered as he headed for the door to find Rose.

Two hours later Val reached for a box on the coffee table. On the lid of the box was written Maggie's collection. Perry Como Christmas music filled the living room space.

"What's in that box, Mommy?"

"Come sit with me on the couch for a minute."

"Okay."

Maggie sat down next to Val.

"Every year since your first Christmas, I have bought a Christmas ornament for you. One day when you are much older than now and have your own place, you will have a good start on your ornament collection. This is very special." Val pulled out the first one.

"Who is this?"

"Minnie Mouse."

"What does it say?"

"Baby's first Christmas."

Val pulled out the second ornament. "What does this one look like?"

"A cannoli."

"I bought that one when we lived in Italy." She got the third one from the box. "This one if from France. Santa Claus standing next to the Eiffel Tower."

"What is the next one?"

"Let's see, who is that?"

"It's Snoopy, he is sitting on top of his doghouse."

"Are you ready to unwrap the one for this year? She handed a small box to Maggie.

Maggie pulled the ornament from the tissue in the box

"It's a Momma and baby penguin."

"Would you like to put them on the tree?"

"Yes."

"Okay, careful. One at a time, okay."

Val's phone rang. She looked at the caller id and saw Amy's name.

"Hi Amy, Congratulations."

"Thank you. I am so excited."

"I know you are. Have you set a date yet?"

"We are thinking about sometime in September."

"That's great." Val started to tear up.

"Are you all right? I heard about James."

"How did you find out?"

"Hal called Ben. Ben told me. He thought you knew, and I didn't know. If I did, I would have told you."

"James should have been the one to tell me. This isn't on you, Ben or anyone else but him."

"What are you going to do?"

"I told him to stay away from me and Maggie."

"I pulled the article up online and read some of the comments people are posting."

"What are they saying?"

"Most of them are saying that people should leave you alone."

"Most?"

"You know the on-line trolls have nothing good to say about anyone."

"I was afraid of that."

"I have a question for you." Amy attempted to change the subject.

"What's that?"

"Could Maggie be in my wedding? We would love for her to be our flower girl."

"That would be great." Val took a deep breath blinking back her tears. "We were going to meet for tea tomorrow and go shopping. Why don't I bring Maggie along and we can look for dresses for her instead?"

"You are keeping Maggie out of school tomorrow?"

"Yeah, just until this blows over."

"Mom wants to start looking for my gown, so okay."

"What are the bridesmaid colors?"

"Red. Maybe a red dress with a white bow for Maggie or vice versa."

"That would be precious. Look I need to hang up, we are decorating our Christmas tree. I'll see you tomorrow at one, okay?"

"Great."

"Hey Pumpkin, guess what? You are going to be a flower girl in Mr. Ben and Miss Amy's wedding."

"Really...What's a flower girl?"

"You get to wear a fancy dress and carry a basket of flowers and throw rose petals down the aisle at the church."

"Throw roses on the floor?"

"Yes."

"Why?"

"To show innocence and love."

"Okay."

"How about we bake cookies after dinner?"

"What's for dinner?"

"Spaghetti and salad."

"Yum."

"Now somewhere in these boxes is our angel and our garland. Let's get moving and finish our tree." Val got up from the couch.

Later that evening Val stood at the kitchen finishing up the dishes. She looked over at Maggie watching a Christmas cartoon. She dried her hands, cautiously picked up her phone and dialed into the diner's voice mail system. The voice came on, "you have ten new messages." She sat on a stool at the counter as message after message came up from reporters, each wanting an exclusive story from her. The last two messages were from a customer wanting special orders. She took a deep breath and looked over at Maggie again.

"What am I going to do?" she whispered.

"What, Mommy?"

"How about a hot chocolate?"

"Yes please."

"Do you want white chocolate or regular chocolate?"

"White chocolate."

"Okay, you do take after your Mama."

James paced back and forth in his room. The anger he felt toward Bryon had not diminished since he saw that article, instead growing stronger.

"How will Val ever trust me again? He mumbled out loud. He lifted the lid on the laptop and opened his banking page.

"That might be enough to last me until I find another job, or freelance for a while, and Mom wants to sell the house."

He opened the file of photos he had stored of Val and Maggie. He stared at the photos he took of Val at the Lights on Festival and touched the screen with his fingertip. Determination took over as he pulled up his email and typed in Bryon's address and in the message he wrote.

"In regard to the story that you want concerning Val Young. I have two words for you. I QUIT."

"Whatever it takes, for Val and Maggie." James walked out of his room and headed for the lobby.

Rose and Hal were seated in the library. Hal was sipping some mulled wine and Rose was trying to concentrate on a book she was reading. She slammed the book shut.

"Give her a little more time," Hal said.

"I know but I am so angry at myself for not telling her the truth."

"That was not yours to tell, and like me, you thought she already knew. So, stop beating yourself up, dear. Besides with all of the social media out there it has been a wonder that things have remained a secret for this long."

"I guess so."

James walked into the room. "I just quit my job," he announced.

"Wow! I got the room fixed up for your Mother and Harvey when they arrive tomorrow. Thank goodness we had a cancelation," Rose said.

"Have you thought about what you are going to do about Val?" Hal asked.

"Stay, and whatever I need to do, I will.

"Have you told your mom yet?" Rose asked

"No, I will tell her tomorrow when she gets here."

"I think that is a move in the right direction," Hal added.

"I am going to have to look for a place to stay since the paper will no longer pay for the hotel room and I don't know about the rental car. I guess I will call them and see if they can put the rest of the time in my name till things settle."

"How much do you know about construction?" Hal asked.

"My father was a construction worker and I put myself through college by rehabbing houses."

Hal looked over at Rose and she smiled.

"How about you stay and work on the house we're buying with Ben on fixing it up. Trade work for a roof over your head?"

"When can I start?"

"The electric company will be out tomorrow to turn the electricity back on. Water should be on tomorrow, too."

"Do you have to pick up your family from the airport?"

"No, Harvey rented a car."

"We have some pieces of old furnishings in the basement that you can use," Rose said.

"Let's go have a look at what tools I have and see if there is anything, I need to order from the hardware store," Hal suggested. He got up and the men headed toward the basement. As soon as they were out of the room Rose picked up her phone and called Val.

Val was sitting at the dining room table, scrolling through the newspaper article and reading the comments people had posted when her phone rang. She looked at the screen and saw Rose's name, sighed and picked up the phone.

"Hi, Rose."

"Hi, how are you?"

"I've been better," Val whispered.

"We are so sorry, as soon as Hal and I found out the truth we told James he had to tell you."

"I know, he told me that. To tell you the truth I was very angry at you and Hal for a little while, but then I realized you were put in a bad spot too."

"Does Maggie know?"

"No, I am keeping her home from school tomorrow."

"Why?"

"So far eight reporters have left messages on the restaurant's voicemail all wanting their piece of meat from me. This is all happening again. I wanted to grab her and run. Get on the first plane out of here. But I can't do that, or maybe I can. I don't know. I am afraid that reporters will show up at her school. I have been reading what people are posting online."

"I saw some of those things also."

"How can people write such lies about me keeping Maggie from her grandparents and making comments that Rich should never have married me in the first place and that I am a gold digger?"

"Val, people who are important to you; they know the truth."

"Someday my daughter might read these things, her friends may see them."

"Val, you can't protect her from everything, and your life is here. Besides if you leave and close the diner, Chris, Amy, Thomas and everybody who works for you would lose their jobs. Everybody here who loves you would be so devastated if you leave. Even Mr. Jeffers."

"I just don't know what to do."

"I know you are closed tomorrow. How about you and I meet up in the morning at the diner and we will talk."

"All right. We are meeting Amy at one o'clock at the bridal store. How about we meet you at eleven."

"Okay."

"Rose, park in the lot behind the diner."

"Got it."

A few minutes later when James and Hal walked back into the room, Rose looked up at them. "James you need to know something."

"What?"

"Reporters have been leaving messages on Val's answering machine at the diner. They all want some type of exclusive."

"I was afraid of that."

"Val is scared they will show up at Maggie's school. People are posting vicious lies about her online, also. Will this all blow over quickly?"

"Probably not, this is usually a slow time of year for news with it being the holidays and the congress and government shutting down for the holidays. They won't stop until she gives an interview to someone."

"Can you do anything to stop it?" Hal asked.

"I can put something out on my own Facebook page about what happened with Bryon editing the story and using the pictures without my knowledge or Val permission."

"Will that stop them?'

"Probably not but I can try."

"It is a step in the right direction." Hal said.

"I don't believe Val will see it that way."

Pulling into her parking spot behind the diner a few minutes before eleven, Val looked around to see if she could spot any reporters. She grabbed her phone from her purse and dialed Rose's number.

"Hello, I am on my way now."

"Do me a favor drive around the front of the diner and see if you spot any reporters."

"Will do."

"Mommy, why are we still outside?" Maggie asked.

"We are waiting for Mrs. Rose."

"Oh, is she going to be a flower girl too?"

"No honey."

A few minutes later Rose parked her car next to Val's van. She got out of the car and walked around to the driver's side door. Val rolled down the window.

"There were four of them across from the diner. Mr. Jeffers was yelling at them to get off his property, or he would call the police," Rose whispered.

"Let's go inside and sit in my office."

Rose heard a vehicle approaching. "Wait a minute." She saw the sign on the side of the truck as it parked next to hers.

"Do you know someone from Kirks and Son's?" she asked.

"Oh, that is my food vendor. I forgot he was coming today."

"Let's get inside before Maggie gets cold."

Val quickly got Maggie out of the car and managed to get them inside without incident.

"Maggie, go sit in Mommy's office for a few minutes, okay?"

"Yes, ma'am."

There was a knock on the back door and Val jumped.

"It's the vendor," Rose said.

"Right."

"Come on Maggie, let's go to your Mom's office."

Val watched them walk into her office and then she turned around and opened the back door.

"Good morning," the man said.

"Look I have appointments today, so let's just get everything inside quickly and I can check the order later."

"Are you sure?" the delivery driver asked.

"Yes."

Val stood hidden from the doorway as he began bringing in the food order. She grabbed the first few boxes and headed for the storage room. Then she grabbed a few more and headed for the freezer. She kept that up until the last of the load was brought in.

"Goodbye Ms. Val," the driver said. "Call me if there are any problems with this order."

"I will, goodbye."

Val followed him to the backdoor and locked it after he left. She quickly put the last of the items away. She walked over to the office door, took a deep breath to calm herself, and opened the door. Maggie was on the couch showing Rose her brand-new Dr. Seuss book.

"I used to read that book to my daughter." Rose said.

"Really?"

"I like the Cat in the Hat. He is funny."

"Maggie, I need to talk to Mrs. Rose for a minute. Can you stay here for a little while longer and read your books?"

"Okay."

"We will be right outside in the kitchen."

Rose and Val walked out of the room but left the door slightly ajar.

Val pulled two stools out from under a metal counter and Rose sat down.

"Would you like a cup of coffee?"

"No, I am fine. But you, on the other hand, look like you could use one."

"I haven't slept at all. I checked the messages this morning from home. There are seven more from reporters. My head hurts."

"You should know that I spoke to James last night about that and he said they will probably stick around till someone gets an exclusive."

"Great. Just great. Mine and Maggie's life gets tossed inside out because of James and his boss."

"James made a mistake, granted and he lied. But answer me something didn't you ask him what he did for a living?"

"This is my fault now?"

"No, but weren't you the least bit curious?"

"I assumed he was a tourist. I don't' know. It never came up. I just want to leave here and get away from them. All the memories came back last night like some sort of mudslide happening in my mind. Rich's death, the funeral, and the custody battle."

"Val I am going to say something that is going to be hard for you to hear, but what did you expect? You have been very lucky that this story hasn't broken before. The granddaughter of a very famous wealthy family and heir apparent to a fortune. All the tourists that come in here and post things on social media. You want to run away but that won't solve anything for you or Maggie. It will only teach her fear."

"Social media is far different than a reporter doing it and getting national exposure. I trusted him. I told him things about myself. I almost…"

"What?"

"It doesn't matter."

"You were falling for him. Everyone could see it."

"Heir apparent. You know the funny thing. I send Rich's mother pictures of Maggie, invitations to her birthday parties, and Christmas. The only thing I have heard back from them was a letter from their attorney, letting me know that they cut Maggie out of their will. What type of Grandparents do that? People online say I am depriving them of being with their granddaughter," Val said trying to change the subject and fight back the tears. "The girl from the wrong side of the tracks. I guess my daughter is guilty by association in their minds. That is how little they loved their son."

"James quit his job last night."

"Why would he do that, he got his big story."

"He never wanted to hurt you."

"I can't trust him, Rose."

"Another hard truth is that you love him."

"He broke my heart. I could never trust him again."

"You know what I love about Festive, beyond all of the fun and festivals is that this is a town that believes in second chances and miracles. You believe in that too; I know you do. Are you going to let Maggie go to school tomorrow?"

"Jeanie's Mom is going to pick her up at the house, and the principal is going to make sure no press or photographers are hanging around outside the school."

"Are you going to open the diner tomorrow?"

"I guess so,"

"Good. Now be strong for you and for Maggie. Think about giving one exclusive to a reporter, telling the whole story. That may be the only way to get rid of the rest of them. Most of all forgive James."

"I will think about it. That is all I can promise."

"Good. I must go pick out paint colors for the cottage. By the way, since James is out of work he is going to be staying there and fixing up the place. A work for rent situation."

"Oh, have fun picking out paint colors."

"I wouldn't dare let Hal pick them out. He can't match his clothes half the time."

Val smiled.

"There we go, I got a little smile out of you. We are here for you whatever you need." Rose got up walked over to Val and hugged her. "You are from the right side of the tracks." She whispered.

Val locked the door behind Rose then walked back into the office.

"Hey Snickerdoodle, what do you want for lunch?"

"Grilled cheese sandwich."

"Alrighty then, One grilled cheese for the flower girl."

James was tearing out the bathroom flooring when he heard the door to the cottage open. He got up, walked into the living room, and was surprised when he saw Wallace Simpson standing there.

"Hello, Wallace,"

"I was up at the Inn and Hal told me you were here working with Ben."

"Yeah, if you need to speak with Ben he will be back later. He's at the hardware store with Rose picking out paint and flooring for this place. I can tell him you stopped by."

"Actually, I am here to speak with you." He moved a little closer to James.

"Why is that?"

"I read the posting you put on your Facebook page this morning. Before I moved back to Festive, I used to be a reporter for a newspaper in Cleveland, Ohio. I know what it feels like to have your boss add information into one of your stories. I have often wished that I had the fortitude to leave that job sooner than I did."

"Yeah, I will need to find a new job soon."

"I read all of the stories you wrote about Festive plus a few other ones. You are a good reporter."

"Correction, I was a good reporter."

"I have a proposition for you."

"I'm listening."

Val was with Amy, Maggie and Amy's mother and the salesperson at the bridal store looking at flower girl dresses.

"What about this one?" Amy pulled out one with spaghetti straps.

"Does it come in red?" her mother asked.

"The sash does." Amy sighed.

"I don't know about those straps on a little girl," her mother added.

"You know we have some beautiful mother of the bride dresses that just came in. Have you thought about what color you want to wear?" the salesperson gestured for Amy's mother to look at another rack.

"Well I was thinking about silver or gold since Amy wants to have an evening wedding."

"We have some excellent gowns for you to choose from."

"Promise me you won't make any decisions till I see it."

"I promise, Mom."

"Have you thought about where you are going to have the reception?" Val asked.

"Yeah, I want to have it at the Chamber of Commerce. My Mom wants to have it at the ballroom, but I think it is kind of tacky."

"The gold wallpaper and mirrors."

"I have been to a couple of receptions at the Chamber and they were always very nice."

"What type of gown do you want?"

"Did you see the ball gown in the window?"

"The one with the lace top and cap sleeves?"

"Yes"

"That gown is beautiful. You should try it on."

"Do you think it is too early to order a dress?"

"Not these days."

"Well let's look for one for Maggie then I will try it on and maybe a few others."

Val smiled for a moment, thumbed through a few more dresses, and pulled out a gown with a satin top and tulle skirt. "How about this one?"

"That is cute."

"Hey pumpkin, let's try this one on and the one with the spaghetti straps." They headed for the dressing room.

Amy sat down on the couch, pulled out her phone and checked her Facebook page. She saw a posting on her feed.

"Wow."

A few minutes later Val and Maggie emerged from the dressing room in the dress Val picked out.

"That is so cute, she looks like a princess," Amy said.

"I am a princess." Maggie looked at herself in the mirror and twirled around.

"Val you need to see this."

"What is it?"

"Something that James posted."

Val reluctantly took Amy's phone and read the message.

"Hello Everyone, I wanted to let you all know that I resigned from my job last night. I could no longer work for a company that allowed my supervisor to add information to my story regarding Val Young and her daughter, especially since Ms. Young was unaware of the article or that I am a reporter. I deeply regret any pain that I have caused her, and I ask that everyone including other reporters respect her privacy."

Val looked over at Maggie as she twirled around again. She gave Amy her phone back.

"Come on, princess, let's go try the other dress on."

Amy got up from the couch and walked over to the salesgirl.

"I want to try that gown on," she pointed to the one in the window.

Cℐ℘Chapter Seventeen℘℃

Just before 5:00 p.m. James' mother and Harvey walked into the lobby of the hotel. She was wearing a red coat and black dress pants. Harvey was about five feet eight inches tall, grey thinning hair and he had on a half-zipped black jacket and khaki pants, a white shirt with a red Christmas bow tie.

"Harvey, I tell you this place looks like a giant Christmas Card."

She walked into the living room. "That fireplace is gorgeous."

Rose walked out of the dining room carrying a platter of cookies.

"Good evening, you must be James's mother and Harvey."

"Anna Hawk and Harvey Williamson."

"Hello, I am going to put these cookies on the buffet in the living room. We have hot apple cider if you would like some, and I will be right back to check you in."

James walked into the lobby his clothes covered with sawdust and paint splatters.

"Mom, Harvey. How was your trip?"

Anna turned and saw all the dust. "Fine, but are you a construction worker now?"

"No, I am just helping out a friend."

"I did a few construction jobs in my day," Harvey added as he reached out to shake James' hand. James smiled and shook his hand.

"Thank you for taking care of things for my Mom."

"Anything for my Anna."

James swallowed hard at the words, my Anna.

"James, why don't you go get our luggage out of the car."

Harvey handed him the keys.

"Which one is it?"

"The red Chrysler 300."

"I'll be right back." James headed out the door for the parking lot.

Rose walked over to the desk. "You were lucky, we had a last-minute cancelation. All the hotels are full up this time of year. You have adjoining rooms 11 and 12. Just go to the top of the stairs and turn right. Now we are having a special dinner for all our guests this evening, if you would like to join us. Dinner will be at 6:00 p.m. in the dining room. We have guests from Britain, and we wanted to surprise them with a traditional English Christmas dinner."

"We wouldn't want to intrude."

"It is no intrusion; we always include all of our guests in our dinners. Sort of like a big extended family." Rose gave them a warm smile.

"All right then, it would be nice to meet some of James new friends"

"I will send James up with your luggage then."

"Come on Harvey, let's go freshen up." They headed for the stairs.

After dinner was finished, Anna, Rose and Mrs. Baker gathered in the living room, while the men went into the library. Rose put a log on the fire and used the poker to get it going full blast.

"Nothing like a fire to brighten up the room and make everything better."

"When James was little the apartment his father and I had didn't have a fireplace. James was so worried that Santa would not come, so his Father built a fake fireplace out of wood scrapes from one of the construction sites he was working at. James was as happy as a boy could be. We were so broke but that was a great Christmas."

"I remember mine and Hal's first Christmas, I was pregnant with our daughter. We were so broke that we got our Christmas tree on Christmas Eve, the last one on the lot. We decorated it and Hal was so proud of that tree. It was so dried out that Christmas morning there wasn't a pine needle left on it. We had needles sticking out of our carpet, all over the presents. It was a mess." Rose smiled at that memory.

Anna looked at her hands for a moment. "Tell me something, how bad has my son messed things up with Val Young."

"Bad, but it may be repairable." Rose answered.

"My son was a brilliant student and he's a gifted writer. But when it comes to romance and women, that boy is dumb as a rock. His first wife was a disaster. I tried to tell him that, but would he listen to his mother? No, of course not. He didn't realize that Harvey and I have been dating for months. He must take after his Father. I had to train that one."

"Didn't we all." Mrs. Baker answered.

"Does Val love my son?"

"I believe she does," Mrs. Baker answered. "but she may have a hard time admitting that."

"Tomorrow, I will go visit her at the diner."

"You may have to wade through a sea of reporters."

"Ah, they don't scare me. I have one in the family."

The next morning Val pulled into the parking lot behind the diner. Jeanie's mother had picked up Maggie at the house. Val glanced into her rearview mirror, caught sight of the empty car seat and started to cry. This was the first morning she did not spend breakfast with her daughter. Suddenly a flash caught her by surprise. Oh, great just great. Val almost jumped out of her van and headed for the door, the reporter and photographer chasing after her.

"Val Young, where have you been all of this time? What do you have to say about your pictures being posted? What about your in-laws, are you in touch with them? Do they see Maggie?"

Val put the key in the door and looked away from the flashing camera. As she opened the door, she kept her face turned away from the camera and yelled. "No comment." She slammed the door in their faces.

A few minutes after 8:00 a.m. Mr. Jeffers walked through the front door. He glanced around the room as though looking for Maggie or Val. He slowly hung his coat up on the rack and walked over to the counter, then took a seat.

"Good Morning Amy,"

"Good Morning."

"Those rotten reporters won't leave. They keep blocking my sidewalk."

"Yeah, one basically chased Val into the building this morning."

"Is Maggie here?"

"No."

"Where is Val?"

"In the kitchen."

"That James fellow?"

"I don't know. Our specials are western omelets."

"Don't bother with the specials, I'll just have oatmeal."

Val heard him order and she peered through the kitchen door. She saw Mr. Jeffers sitting in his usual seat with his head down. I know how you feel. Rose's words about an exclusive rang through her brain. She stared at the phone for a moment and picked it up.

"Hello," Wallace answered.

"Hello, Wallace, this is Val. I have an exclusive for you. Can you meet me at the diner?"

Half an hour later, Wallace walked into the diner followed by Anna, Harvey, Rose and Hal. Amy walked over toward the group.

"Hi Wallace, why don't you grab a seat at the counter, and I will be right over for your order. Are you all together?" She pointed to Rose.

"Yes."

She walked the group over to one of the booths by the jukebox. After they sat down, she handed them menus.

"Today's specials are western omelet, spiced pumpkin pecan pancakes with sausage and apple crepes with bacon. What can I get you all to drink this morning?"

Val came out of the kitchen and headed toward Wallace. "Good morning."

"Morning, Val."

"Looks like you get your exclusive, Wallace. One picture of me, no pictures of Maggie and I get a list of all the questions beforehand."

Wallace looked at his hands for a moment.

"Can I get a cup of coffee?"

"What? Oh, of course."

Val poured him a cup of coffee.

"Val, don't be upset, but I have been thinking about this since you called. I am not the one to do this story. I'm just a small-town reporter with a limited readership. No one is going to pay much attention to what I write. I don't think it will help you. Besides I am semi-retired. I worked out a deal with James yesterday, for him to take over the paper."

"You did what?" Val asked.

"Val, don't get mad. I read a lot of his articles and he is very good. The articles he wrote about Festive are first-rate. He really gets what this town is all about. Plus, it took courage and integrity for him to quit like he did. I wish I had that when my boss pulled the same stunt on me. James wants to start over, and I believe he has a chance here to do some good."

"I'll think about it."

Amy walked over to Val.

"Excuse me, Val you have a phone call. It's Mr. Dixon, he said it's important."

"Okay, I will be back."

Val headed for the kitchen.

"Hello Mr. Dixon, what can I help you with?"

"I just wanted to let you know that you have a package at my place. I saw one of those porch pirates at your place. So, I sent Shakespeare and Lola after him. They ran him off. Funny thing is, this one had a camera around his neck."

"Okay thank you for letting me know. If it is okay, I can be there around six to pick up the package."

"Sure."

"And thank you." Val stared at the phone for a moment.

Amy walked into the kitchen and handed her the orders for Rose's table.

"Is everything all right?"

"Yeah, Mr. Dixon saw a reporter at my place skulking around. So, he sent Shakespeare and Lola after him. Shakespeare the lovable Pitbull, that would have licked him to death."

"He had more to fear from Lola. I swear that Chihuahua is possessed," Amy added.

"I'll get these orders up. Tell Wallace I will be out in a minute."

Amy walked toward the dining area. A few minutes later she returned with an order for crepes.

Give him the exclusive, something or else they won't give me a minute of peace. Wallace of all times for you to retire.

A few minutes later Val hit the silver bell. "Orders up Amy."

Thomas knocked on the kitchen door. Val walked over, unlocked the door, and opened it photographers started snapping pictures of her again, and she slammed the door in their faces.

"What is going on?" Thomas wanted to know.

"Did they ask you anything?"

"Yeah one of them wanted to know if I worked here."

"What did you say?"

"I just told him that I am a dishwasher. That's all. They were asking questions about how well I knew you."

"What else did you tell them?"

"She is a nice boss. They are kind of scary people. I mean pushing and shoving."

"That's it."

Val walked into the dining room and she saw Hal and Rose seated at one of the tables with a couple. She headed for Rose's table.

"Good morning everyone."

"Good morning Val." Rose started "This is Anna Hawk, James' mother and her friend Harvey."

Val took a step back for a moment and drew a deep breath. *His mother? What is she doing here?* "Welcome to my diner. Is everything okay with your meal?"

"Harvey and I were just saying these crepes are wonderful. Where did you learn how to make them so light?"

"France. Would you happen to know where your son is? I need to speak to him."

"He was headed over to the cottage to do some work and then out to the Dixon place for his Give Back ticket," Anna answered.

"Okay, thank you. Please enjoy the rest of your meal." Val walked over to the counter area. "Amy, I need a favor from you. Can you and Ben watch Maggie tonight? I have something I need to do."

"Sure."

"I'll call Jeanie's Mom after school and arrange it."

"Val, are you all right?" Mr. Jeffers asked.

"I will be soon, and Wallace?"

Wallace looked up at her.

"I am going to follow your advice."

"Good. Can I order my breakfast now?"

"Amy will get that for you."

A few moments later, she was in her office and grabbed her cell phone out of her purse. She punched in the Dixon's phone number.

"Hello," Mrs. Dixon answered.

"Hello, Mrs. Dixon would James Hawk happen to be there by chance?"

"Yes, He just got here a few minutes ago."

"May I speak to him, please?"

"Sure, honey, hold on"

A few minutes later James came on the line. "Hello Val, are you all right?"

"You can have your exclusive, only if you agree to my rules. I am going to close the diner at six. Meet me here at that time."

"Okay. What are your rules?" he asked.

"One picture of me only. I have to agree to all of the questions, and I see a copy of the article before you put it out."

"All right," James answered. "That sounds fair."

"James, make sure you come in the front entrance."

A few minutes later Val came out of the kitchen carrying Wallace's breakfast. She looked over at Rose's table and saw that Anna was the only one sitting there.

"Here you go, Wallace. On the house today."

"You'll go broke that way." Mr. Jeffers said.

Val turned around.

"I'll be happy though and your granddaughter will be here tomorrow."

"My granddaughter?"

"Yeah, Maggie loves you as much as you love her, and I can't think of a better grandfather for her."

"Thank you. You have made this old man very happy."

"You're not old, remember?"

Val turned and grabbed the coffee pot and walked over toward Anna. "Did everyone desert you?"

"Not exactly, Hal and Rose had an errand to run and I sent Harvey to the florist. I want a Poinsettia plant for our room."

"Would you like a refill?"

"No, but would you sit down for a few minutes and talk with me, please?"

Val hesitated for a moment, but she decided to listen to what Anna had to say.

"Okay," Val set the coffee pot down on the table and took the seat opposite from Anna.

"You must be wondering what I am doing here. After all, my son isn't a teenager."

"The thought crossed my mind."

"I had to see the woman who stole my sons' heart. As a mother, you know how we want to protect our children and we want the best for them."

"Of course, I do."

"I have to tell you; my son is dumb as a rock when it comes to women. I am his mother, so I can say that. His ex-wife only wanted him for the idea of fame and prestige she thought she would get by marrying a reporter. I tell you he must have got that lack of understanding women from his father. My husband, may he rest in peace, was not the most romantic man in the world. For our first anniversary, he bought me a toaster. I wanted to hit him alongside his head with it. But I digress…where was I? Oh yes, James. Where you are concerned my James made a huge mistake. He was torn between what his boss wanted, what he thought I needed, and doing right by you. Yes, he should have told you the truth right away, but my guess is he was afraid of losing you. I wanted to show you something." Anna pulled the newspaper clipping from her purse and puts them on the table. "These are the articles he wrote since coming here. He did not mention you or your daughter once. If he wanted to act like one of those idiots outside, he would have written the article and cut and run. But he stayed and he is here to face the consequences of his actions. No matter what they might be. Maybe he deserves a little forgiveness and a second chance."

"I'll think about it, that is all I can promise right now."

"All right then. I can accept that."

Just then Harvey walked in the door carrying one red poinsettia and one white one.

"This one tries too hard to make me happy, but I have to admit I love it."

Val smiled.

"Well, that is progress. Thank you for taking the time to sit with me."

"You're welcome, By the way, what did your husband get you for your second anniversary?"

"Roses and chocolate."

"Betsy's store down the street has chocolate from Switzerland."

"We will stop there next. Thank you for the tip."

Val watched them walk out the door, smiling at the way they kept touching each other, then she picked up the articles and started to read them.

James walked through the front door of the diner at 6:00 p.m. and immediately noticed Chris standing behind the counter. James was carrying the package Mr. Dixon had rescued from Val's place. Chris glared at him with the force of an angry army brigade. James hung his coat up on the rack and walked toward the counter. He put the package at the end of the counter.

"Is Val here?"

"She is in the back."

"Oh, okay." James sat down.

Chris walked toward him. "Look man, you hurt her. Val is like a sister to me and I don't appreciate when someone hurts my family. Yet for some reason I don't understand why she is letting you have a second chance." Chris unfolded his arms and came closer to James, then leaned over the counter.

"Don't hurt her again." He straightened up, turned and walked over to the kitchen door and pushed it open. "He is here."

Val walked into the dining area. James looked over at her then bowed his head back, unable to look her in the eye.

"Chris you can go home now, I'll lock up."

"Are you sure?"

"Yeah."

He stopped at the front door, and turned around looking at James, "Remember what I said."

"I will."

Chris walked out the door and Val slid the deadbolt in place.

"Would you like some coffee?" she asked.

Val walked over to the counter grabbed a mug and filled it for him.

"How are you?"

"James, really my life has been turned upside down and I haven't had any sleep."

"Val, I know you don't believe me, but I am sorry."

"Do you have your list of questions?"

He pulled out a pad of paper from his pocket and handed it to Val.

"Look, let's go sit at one of the booths." She motioned to one near the jukebox. James followed her over and they sat down opposite each other.

Val looked over the list. She grabbed a pen from her pocket and scratched out a few of the questions. Then she gave the list back to James.

"Remember our deal."

"Yes."

"Ask away then."

"Why did you leave New York?"

"After my husband died and the custody case was over, everybody that knew us did nothing but gossip and spread lies. The reporters would not leave us alone either. They thought Maggie was going to get the Young fortune at some time. They would pounce out of the bushes at us. I couldn't mourn my husband privately as one should. I felt like a prisoner in my own home. So, I packed up and left."

James swallowed hard. "Where did you go?"

"We traveled throughout Europe spending a couple of months at different locations. I learned how to cook different cuisines and spent a lot of time with my daughter."

"Do you hear from Rich's parents?"

"No, they did not approve of our marriage, though I do wish they had some contact with Maggie"

"Why?"

"They are a link to my husband's past."

"Do you try to contact them?"

"Yes, I send his mother emails with Maggie's pictures attached. Invitations to her birthday parties, things like that."

"And they have not responded?"

"Not once. I did receive a letter from their lawyer. Maggie was cut out of their will."

"Why did you settle in Festive?"

"This town is more than the celebrations; people here have a heart. They care for each other. People can rebuild their lives here with the dignity and quiet they need. Many of the tourists that visit year after year have developed relationships with the townsfolk. Sort of like having a large extended family. I wanted that for my daughter, and I needed that for myself. Here we were free to be ourselves; people are treated with respect and kindness. It is a beautiful place with the mountains and the historic town. A soul can recover here."

"What will you do now?"

"Hopefully stay and raise my daughter."

James looked at his coffee mug.

"Is that enough for your story?"

"Yeah," he looked Val in the eyes.

"I want you to tell those other reporters out there, that you got the exclusive. There will be no more interviews or pictures, and to stay away from my home, and my daughter.

Look James, I know now you didn't mean to hurt me or Maggie."

"But I did, and I am so sorry, I just wish I knew how to make it up to you. I do love you, Val and Maggie too."

Val looked at her hands for a moment and she started to cry "The past few days reminded me of something. I used to wish that I could go back and fix one thing in my life, it would be that argument I had with Rich on the day he died. I let my fear of change get in the way of his dreams, and I can never ever change that." She took a deep breath. "Festive is a place for second chances, Rose reminded me of that. Your mother claims I stole your heart and that you are a basic klutz when it comes to relationships. So, I am giving you this one chance to make things right. No more lies, no more omissions, just being straight with one another. Can you promise me that?"

"Yes."

"Please hand me your notebook."

James gave it to her, and Val wrote something down.

"This is my email, please email me a copy of the story tonight. Do you think anyone will pick it up?"

"I have a contact at MSN that will work with me."

"Okay, then that is done. I am going home and hug my daughter." She got up.

"Val. I…"

"Tomorrow's specials are chocolate chip pancakes, French toast with fresh fruit and sausage gravy and biscuits. Why don't you stop in."

"Plus, I am shutting down on the 23rd for the staff Christmas party, if you would like to attend that would be great and bring your Mom and her friend Harvey if they are still in town."

"I think they will be."

"May I walk you to your car?"

"I got that, plus you have some news to deliver to those reporters out front."

They walked over to the coat rack and James helped Val with her coat.

James put on his coat and Val saw a look of pain on his face as James rubbed his shoulder.

"What happened?"

"I was chopping wood for most of the day at the Dixons." James looked at Val. 'I don't know how to thank you."

"Tonight, we start over. Goodnight James."

"Goodnight."

She locked the door after him and watched for a moment as he walked across the street and headed for the group of reporters still camped out on Mr. Jeffers's lawn. Crossing over the floor she picked up the large package on the counter and headed out the back door. I can drop Carrie's father's gifts on the way home. Thank goodness I had them gift wrapped already.

ᐸChapter Eighteenᐳ

V al, Maggie and James arrived at the diner a few minutes before the staff Christmas party was to begin. The night before Val and James decorated a special Santa chair for Hal to sit in for their next secret elf mission. Luckily the reporters left town the day after James told them he would be sending out the only exclusive. Most of them were already chasing another story about some actress getting married.

Val and James were balancing trays of food on their arms as they walked in the door.

"Where do you want me to put this?" James asked.

"On the counter, Maggie please hang up your coat and then sit down for a few minutes while Mr. James and I set everything up, Okay?"

"Yes, ma'am."

"Can you bring in the rest of the food James? I will get the punch and the hot chocolate going. Plus, I have to get the desserts out of the refrigerator."

"Got it."

Val walked over to the jukebox and punched in some numbers. Nat King Cole's version of *The Christmas Song* filled the air.

"Make a space for the crown roast, stuffing, lasagna, roasted sweet potatoes with squash and cranberry agrodolce, mashed potatoes, tossed salad, rolls, salad dressings, homemade applesauce, the Italian dream cake, Christmas cake and Mexican wedding cookies will go on the side table with the punch and hot chocolate."

"Mommy, who are you talking too?"

"Myself honey, people do that when they get older."

"That's weird."

You don't know the half of It, kiddo."

James came back in carrying more food.

"I have one more trip to make. I think you have enough food to feed the whole county."

Just then they heard a tapping on the front door. Val turned around and saw Amy and Ben standing there. She walked over to them and unlocked the door.

"We thought you could use some help," Amy said.

"Yes, I sure can."

"Go ahead tell her the news."

"What news?"

"Ben is buying Betsy's store. He is going to start his remodeling combo landscaping business and he already has a contract with Maryland State University to do some work on the building they are taking over."

"That is fantastic news."

"Yeah and we are going to rent out the apartment above the store."

"You may want to speak with James about that, he is looking for a place."

"I think I will."

"Amy, will you set out the dishes while I get everything else going?"

"Got it."

About a half an hour later all the guests arrived including Thomas, his mother, brothers and sisters. Anna and Harvey walked into the front door.

"Harvey, look at all of this food."

"Everything smells great."

"Hi Mom, Harvey," James walked across the room. "Let me hang up your coats."

"Everything looks wonderful," Anna said.

"Everything is wonderful," James replied.

"With Val?"

"We are working things out, Ma, at her speed."

"Okay then."

Val walked into the room wearing a red sweater with a black mid-length skirt and ankle boots.

Anna looked at James and then at Val.

"She is beautiful."

"Yes, she is." James added.

Chris walked into the room from the kitchen door. He was wearing a dress shirt, blue jeans and cowboy boots.

Val looked at them and smiled, then clapped her hands to gain everyone's attention "Hello, everyone. Come on in and there is plenty of food, please help yourself. Santa will be arriving soon."

"Santa is coming?" Maggie asked.

Rose walked into the room from the kitchen entrance.

"I think he may be here. Let me check, I will be right back."

Val walked into the kitchen and saw Hal dressed in his red and white Santa suit.

"Is everything ready for operation, Santa?"

"Yes, I have elves waiting at the toy store and the clothing store," Val answered.

"Well I got a Christmas tree and decorations in the truck already, so let's go."

Hal came through the kitchen door into the dining area, and then stopped.

"Ho, Ho, Ho, Merry Christmas."

"Santa!" The kids yelled.

"Okay, kids everyone gets a turn to sit on Santa's lap and tell him what you want for Christmas."

One by one the kids met with Santa while Rose texted their wish lists to the appropriate stores. Operation Surprise Santa was underway.

Val waited until the last child had finished talking to Santa and then she approached him with a few envelopes. "Santa, I need your help. Would you do the honor of giving each one of my staff their Christmas gifts?"

"It would be a pleasure." Hal made his way around the room giving out each one of the cards according to what name was written on the envelope. After he finished, he turned to the group. "I have to head back to the North Pole now; I have a big night coming up soon."

"Goodbye Santa."

About an hour later as Val, Amy and James were cleaning up the diner, when the phone rang. Val picked it up.

"Hello?"

"Ms. Val this is Thomas."

"Thank you for the gift card to the grocery store and the bonus. When we got home there was a Christmas tree and presents on the front porch."

"Really, who are they from?"

"The tags say Merry Christmas from Santa and the elves. My Mom is so happy, and my brothers and sisters are dancing in the living room."

"Merry Christmas, Thomas."

"Merry Christmas, ma'am."

Christmas Eve, the town square was overflowing with family members, tourists, friends of the school kids and choir members. James and Val stood next to each other. Rose, Hal, Anna, Harvey, and the Bakers were a few rows behind the two them. The multi-church choir started singing *O Come All Ye Faithful*. Val looked at James and smiled. She gently slipped her arm in his and laid her head against his shoulder. Tears burned her eyes when James smiled.

Rose tapped Anna's arm and pointed toward the couple, "Well look at that handsome couple."

"Took them long enough."

The children soon took to the stage and they started telling the story of Christ's birth. Jeanie and Maggie stood side by side on the stage. Val said a little prayer as Maggie's turn to say her line came up.

"This will be a sign to you ... you will find the baby wrapped in swaddling clothes and lying in a manger," Maggie spoke very loudly.

Val resisted the urge to clap right then "Way to go baby girl," she whispered.

Early Christmas morning, Maggie opened all her Christmas presents from Santa and she was very happy with the array of toys and clothes that she received. Then Val showed Maggie how to make her favorite Nantucket cranberry pie.

Christmas afternoon Mr. Jeffers, James, Anna and Harvey arrived filling Val's living room.

"I can't believe you cooked a huge meal the other day and found the time to make another meal today," Anna said. "Thank you for inviting us again. You make us feel like family."

"You are welcome, and you are my family now. Everyone please gather around; it is time to open the other Christmas presents. Val sat down on the couch next to James.

"Mommy, can I be Santa?"

"Yes, you can."

"How about you start with the gift for Mr. Jeffers?"

"Okay," Maggie pulled a big box from underneath the tree.

"Here you go, Mr. Jeffers." she handed it to him.

"Did you wrap this yourself?"

"Mommy helped a little. Go ahead open it."

He lifted the lid and pulled out a new brown wool coat.

"Do you like it? I picked it out."

"I love it. Thank you."

"Who is next, Mommy?"

"Mrs. Anna and Mr. Harvey."

Maggie looked around the tree and pulled out two small boxes.

"Here you go," She handed the boxes to them.

"Thank you, Santa," Anna replied.

They opened their boxes at the same time and pulled out Christmas ornaments.

"For your first Christmas in your new place," Val said.

"Who is next, Mommy?"

"Mr. James."

Maggie picked up his gift and handed it to him.

"Thank you, Santa."

"This is fun."

James opened the box and pulled out a wooden nameplate for his desk. He looked at the gold piece and read aloud, "James Hawk Editor and Chief. Thank you, Val."

"Mommy here is your gift from me." Maggie handed her a small box.

Val opened it and pulled out a silver charm bracelet. The charm attached said World's Best Mom.

"Come here munchkin." Val hugged Maggie.

"Santa," James started I have a gift for your Mom. "May I give it to her now?"

"Okay."

James walked over to the tree and pulled out a small package. He handed the gift to Val and sat back down next to her on the couch.

Val opened the box and lifted out a gold necklace with a blue sapphire pendant attached to it.

"James this is beautiful."

"Here let me put help you with that."

Val lifted her hair up off her neck and James put the chain around her neck.

"I can't believe you did that."

"I am not a complete romantic klutz."

"That's all the gifts," Maggie announced.

"Not all." Val got up off the couch.

"Have a seat on the couch pumpkin. This Santa has to go down the hallway and get this one."

Maggie sat down on the couch as Val headed for the guest room.

A few minutes later Val emerged cradling a very tiny dachshund puppy.

Maggie started to cry as Val put the puppy in her lap.

"Can I keep it?"

"Yes, you can keep her."

"Thank you, Mommy."

Later that evening after Anna, Harvey and Mr. Jeffers had left, Val and James walked down the hall to Maggie's room. They opened the door and found Maggie soundly asleep in her bed. The puppy Daisy lay snoring in the doggy bed in the corner.

They headed for the living room and sat down on the couch.

"This was a great Christmas," James said.

"It's not over yet" Val reached for a small wrapped package on the coffee table and handed it to James.

"What's this?"

"Open it."

He opened it and pulled out a sprig of mistletoe then smiled.

He held it over Val's head and leaned forward and she moved forward.

They kissed slowly, long and lasting.

After the kiss, Val curled her feet up on the couch, held safe in his arms. "Merry Christmas, I love you so much, James."

"I love you, Val. Merry Christmas."

About the Author

S andy's interests in writing blossomed after one of her English professors gave the final assignment to either write five poems or recite Hamlet's "To be or not to be" speech. After completing the five poems, she continued to write poetry and perform at open mic nights. Several years ago she read about an article in the local newspaper concerning a challenge to write a novel in one month, Sandy pushed herself to completing that task, and after that she fell in love with creating the entire story and each one of the characters that real people could relate to.

Sandy is the youngest of five children and she grew up in the quiet area of Pasadena, Maryland. A small town where one could catch a bushel of blue crabs from the Magothy River in the morning, steam them in afternoon while having one's friends over to watch football. Her mother always has a way of making Christmas special, so Sandy is that person who is in the Christmas mode 90% of the time. While she currently resides in Oklahoma. Maryland will always be her hearts home.

Sandy's hobbies include perusing Pinterest for new recipes to make (especially holiday desserts}, collecting teapot Christmas ornaments, reading, watching football and hunting for that perfect coffee shop to relax in and of course anything and everything Christmas related.

CPSIA information can be obtained
at www.ICGtesting.com
Printed in the USA
FSHW022055200520
70335FS